Cognitive Behavioural Therapy: A Very Short Introduction

VERY SHORT INTRODUCTIONS are for anyone wanting a stimulating and accessible way into a new subject. They are written by experts, and have been translated into more than 45 different languages.

The series began in 1995, and now covers a wide variety of topics in every discipline. The VSI library currently contains over 700 volumes—a Very Short Introduction to everything from Psychology and Philosophy of Science to American History and Relativity—and continues to grow in every subject area.

Very Short Introductions available now:

For more information visit our website

www.oup.com/vsi/

Freda McManus

COGNITIVE BEHAVIOURAL THERAPY

A Very Short Introduction

OXFORD
UNIVERSITY PRESS

OXFORD
UNIVERSITY PRESS

Great Clarendon Street, Oxford, OX2 6DP,
United Kingdom

Oxford University Press is a department of the University of Oxford.
It furthers the University's objective of excellence in research, scholarship,
and education by publishing worldwide. Oxford is a registered trade mark of
Oxford University Press in the UK and in certain other countries

© Freda McManus 2022

The moral rights of the author have been asserted

First edition published in 2022

Impression: 1

Published in the United States of America by Oxford University Press
198 Madison Avenue, New York, NY 10016, United States of America

British Library Cataloguing in Publication Data
Data available

Library of Congress Control Number: 2021949073

ISBN 978-0-19-875527-2

Printed in Great Britain by
Ashford Colour Press Ltd, Gosport, Hampshire

In memory of Vincent James McManus, 1947–2019, in recognition of his love of learning and teaching.

Contents

Preface

This book aims to introduce cognitive behaviour therapy (CBT) which is the name used to refer to a range of therapies that share an underpinning model of cognition (thought) and behaviour as being central in understanding and resolving psychological distress. The aim of this book is to give information about CBT rather than to teach you how to practice it or to be a self-help manual—see the Further reading section for books that fulfil those functions. Instead, this book gives a succinct overview of what CBT is, how it developed, what it is used for, with whom, and potential future challenges and areas of development.

List of illustrations

List of tables

Chapter 1
The behavioural origins of CBT

The role of behaviour in determining emotional responses has long been recognized. Aristotle declared in his *Nicomachean Ethics* that, 'It is through acting bravely that we become brave', while Johann Wolfgang von Goethe (1749–1832) noted that 'to heal psychic ailments...the understanding avails nothing, reasoning little, time much, but resolute action everything.'

And that is the fundamental idea behind cognitive behavioural therapies, or CBT—that our cognitions (thoughts or other mental events) and behaviours influence the way we feel, and vice versa. That thoughts and feelings mediate between what happens to us and our response to it. For example, Jack and Jill are both scratched by a cat as children. Jack goes on to develop a phobia of cats but Jill does not. There are any number of variables contributing to why they responded so differently, including biological factors such as genetic vulnerability to anxiety, and environmental and sociocultural factors such as exposure to other cats, and the roles of cats in their culture. However, it may be that through careful examination of Jack's thoughts about cats and behaviour towards them we have the opportunity to ameliorate his phobia.

In recent years, CBT has become the dominant model of psychological therapy in both the UK and the USA and its use is becoming ever more widespread. The evidence for its effectiveness is sufficient for it to be a recommended intervention for most common mental health problems in the UK government's National Institute for Clinical Excellence Guidelines (https://www.nice.org. uk). However, part of the reason for CBT's success is its ability to evolve, which it continues to do. So CBT today is different from how it was a decade or two, ago and the same is likely to be true in another decade or two. Given the breadth of CBT, and its continuing development, this book will first focus on traditional CBT, developed by Albert Ellis and Aaron Beck in the 1950s, 1960s, and 1970s. Later chapters will then look at how traditional CBT has evolved and been adapted for use in different settings and contexts, and what challenges it may face in the coming years.

Historically CBT grew out of theories about how we learn, particularly about how behaviours are learned, and from the work of several psychologists who studied the cognitive processes that underlie how we perceive the world, how we reason, and how we remember. Prior to the 1950s, the psychodynamic psychotherapy of Sigmund Freud was the dominant model of psychotherapy. But Freudian psychoanalysis focused on unobservable processes that happen within the mind, which meant that it was not amenable to measurement, and so largely untestable—there was no way of assessing evidence for its theoretical basis or its effectiveness. Hence, its usefulness was questioned by scientific psychology, which objected to the lack of observable, measurable processes and outcomes. As a result, behaviour therapy arose from scientific psychology. The behavioural approach took the view that since what went on in a person's mind was unobservable and thus not amenable to scientific study, all unconscious (unobservable) processes could be ignored, and instead it concentrated on studying observable behaviour and on developing theories to explain how that behaviour was learned (learning theory).

Behavioural and learning theorists studied the associations between observable events, particularly *stimuli* (some aspect of the environment) and *responses* (observable or measurable reactions from the person or animal being studied) to understand how people learn new associations between stimuli and responses—for example, how people develop fears of harmless objects. The aim was to use theories of how people learn in order to modify unwanted emotional or behavioural responses such as fear. Instead of viewing phobias as a defence against the anxiety of repressed impulses, as Freud had, they viewed them as learned associations. So phobias were seen as responses that were learned either through direct experience or via some form of observation or instruction. If phobias were a learned response, then it logically follows that what can be learned can be unlearned.

Behavioural theorists used animals to scientifically study learning and identified three main types of learning. The first is *classical conditioning*, which is learning that depends on associations between events, such as feeling hungry when you hear the dinner bell because you have come to associate it with mealtimes. The second is *operant conditioning*, which is learning that depends on the consequences of behaviour, so positive consequences lead to the behaviour being repeated and negative consequences reduce the frequency of the behaviour. Examples of these are learning not to touch hot things because it hurts and working in order to gain money. The final form of learning, *observational learning*, is learning by watching others, such as learning to use a computer game by watching someone else playing it.

Classical conditioning

Classical conditioning is the learning that occurs when two stimuli are repeatedly paired—that is, they happen simultaneously. A response which is at first elicited by the second stimulus comes to be elicited by the first stimulus alone. Classical conditioning involves three stages and at each stage the stimuli and responses involved are given specific scientific names.

Stage 1: Before conditioning. This stage focuses on the natural relationship that exists between a stimulus and a response. These are called unconditioned stimuli and responses as they are not associations that have been learned (conditioned), but are natural responses. So a stimulus in the environment produces a response which is a natural reaction to that stimulus. For example, the unconditioned stimulus (UCS) of chocolate produces an unconditioned response (UCR) of pleasure. Or a UCS of a dog bite produces a UCR of pain. The second stimulus involved in this stage is called the neutral stimulus (NS) and could be any stimulus (e.g. a colour, sound, object) that, at this stage, does not produce any response.

Stage 2: During conditioning. The process of conditioning is when the neutral stimulus (NS) becomes associated with the unconditioned stimulus (UCS), at which point it becomes known as the conditioned stimulus (CS). For this association to be made the unconditioned stimulus must be associated with the neutral/conditioned stimulus a number of times. If you repeatedly associate an unconditioned stimulus (UCS) such as a dog bite with an neutral stimulus (the dog), eventually the neutral stimulus (the dog) will become associated with the unconditioned response of pain, even in the absence of the unconditioned stimulus (the bite). Such associations usually take many pairings of the neutral and unconditioned stimuli but can be learnt from only one pairing of the stimuli if the response is a novel, or especially pleasurable or aversive, one. For example, if you are violently ill after eating a specific food (which was previously an neutral stimulus), especially if it is the first time you have eaten that food (i.e. it is novel), you are highly likely to feel sick at the thought of that food, regardless of whether it was the cause of the original sickness.

Stage 3: After conditioning. Now the conditioned (previously neutral) stimulus (CS) has been associated with the unconditioned stimulus (UCS) to create a new conditioned response (CR). The Russian physiologist Ivan Pavlov famously demonstrated the

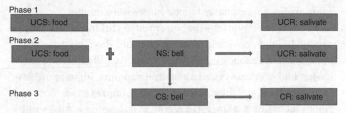

1. Diagram to show classical conditioning.

process of classical conditioning when he conditioned dogs to salivate at the sound of a bell by repeatedly pairing the bell with feeding them. The natural association was for the dogs to salivate in response to seeing their food, but after repeatedly pairing the sight of their food with the sound of the bell, the dogs began to salivate at the sound of the bell only, demonstrating that they had learned a new association between what had previously been a neutral stimulus (the bell) and an unconditioned response (salivation) (Figure 1). An everyday example of this is when my cat comes running when she hears me open the door to the cupboard in which her food is kept. The fact that she doesn't come when I open other cupboard doors means that she shows *stimulus discrimination*—that is, she has learned to respond differently to various stimuli that are similar. The same principles underlie pet training aids such as anti-bark collars or electric fences—the animal associates that area of the garden with pain, so learns to avoid the area.

Once this classical conditioning, or learning by association, had been demonstrated in animals the next challenge was to see if it also applied to humans. The infamous, and now ethically questionable, demonstration of this was John Watson and Rosalie Rayner's description from 1920 of conditioning a fear of white rats in a 9- to 12-month-old boy known as 'Little Albert'.

Everyday observations of children led American psychologists John Broadus Watson and Rosalie Rayner to hypothesize that children's fearful responses to loud noises were innate unconditioned responses—that most young children inherently respond to loud noises with fear. Watson and Rayner wanted to find out if this unconditioned fear response could be conditioned to what had previously been an neutral stimulus. First, in order to establish a baseline, they tested Albert's responses to various stimuli including a white rat, a rabbit, and a monkey. Albert did not show fear connected to any of these stimuli but did cry in response to loud noises. During the experiment, a white rat was placed near Albert and he was encouraged to play with it. Every time Albert touched the rat, the experimenters made a loud noise. Albert responded to the noise by crying and showing fear. After several such pairings of the two stimuli (rat and noise), Albert began to show fear and to cry in response to the rat, even without the accompanying loud noise. The rat, originally a neutral stimulus, had become a conditioned stimulus, and was eliciting a conditioned response similar to the distress (unconditioned response) originally shown in response to the loud noise (unconditioned stimulus). Albert also showed some fear of other furry white animals, which means he showed *stimulus generalization*, which is the opposite of my cat's stimulus discrimination, and occurs when the organism demonstrates the conditioned response to other stimuli that are similar to the conditioned stimulus. Watson and Rayner had shown that classical conditioning could be used to create fear linked to an object that was previously not feared. Indeed, they had created a phobia—that is, an irrational fear that is out of proportion to the danger that the object presents. Over the next few weeks Albert was observed and ten days after the conditioning his fear of the rat was much less. This dying out of a learned response is called *extinction*. But there is also a phenomenon of *spontaneous recovery*—the reappearance of an extinguished conditioned response when the conditioned stimulus returns after a period of absence. So there is no guarantee that his fear of rats or similar objects would not return at some point in the future.

While Watson and Raynor showed that they could use the principles of classical conditioning to induce fear where it would not otherwise have been, there is no record of them trying to reverse the fear. Inspired by Watson and Raynor's work, the American psychologist Mary Cover Jones was the first to try to use the same methods to reduce fear, in the 1920s. Peter was a 3-year-old boy with a naturally occurring phobia of rabbits that had generalized to similar stimuli. Jones used the principles of classical conditioning to reduce his fear by doing roughly the opposite of what Watson and Raynor had done with Albert. She gradually introduced Peter to rabbits while pairing the experience with a pleasant stimulus (sweets). First the rabbit was kept at a distance from Peter and then it was gradually brought closer, while he was given sweets. The result was that his fear in response to both rabbits and similar stimuli diminished. However, we do not know what the long-term outcome was.

The development of behaviour therapy

In the 1960s therapists began to utilize these methods to help patients overcome fears. The task of therapy was to help the patient establish a new non-fearful response to the previously feared stimulus. This could be done in a variety of ways. Most common was *systematic desensitization* or *graduated exposure therapy*, which is a form of *counter conditioning* developed by the South African psychiatrist Joseph Wolpe in the 1950s. This makes use of *reciprocal inhibition*, in which a response is inhibited because it is incompatible with another response. In the case of phobias, fear involves tension and tension is incompatible with relaxation. So relaxation skills are used to inhibit the anxious response. Systematic desensitization uses the gradually increasing exposure that Jones employed with Peter. This means getting the patient to construct a hierarchy of their feared situations starting with situations that would only bother them a little and working up to full exposure to the phobic stimulus or situations that they are most fearful of. Initially the patient is exposed to the anxiety-producing stimulus at a low level, and this level of exposure is maintained until the fear reduces due to both reciprocal inhibition and *habituation*, which is the natural diminishing of a response to a stimulus that is presented repeatedly without change (e.g. how we eventually stop noticing the hum of a new fridge or the ticking of a new clock), such that anxiety dissipates over time. Once the anxiety is significantly reduced, the patient can be exposed to a slightly more potent version of the stimulus. This continues until the patient no longer feels anxious. Such graduated exposure can also be combined with relaxation to accelerate the habituation by also using reciprocal inhibition.

Example of a hierarchy for a spider phobia

Situation	Anxiety rating
Large spider crawling on my neck	100
Large spider on my arm	95
Large spider on my trouser leg	90
Medium spider on my face	90
Holding glass jar with large spider in it, without top on jar	70
Large spider being loose on other side of the room	65
Holding glass jar with large spider in it, with top on jar	60
Holding glass jar with medium spider in it, without top on jar	50
Tiny spider on my neck	40
Tiny spider on my hand	35
Watching video of large spiders	35
Looking at photos of large spiders	25
Thinking or talking about spiders	20

While systematic desensitization was a significant advance in the treatment of phobias it is not without its challenges. Patients may struggle to implement or benefit from the relaxation strategies, or to make accurate predictions about the level of anxiety that they will feel in a particular situation. Furthermore, not all phobias are amenable to systematic exposure in a controlled manner, for example, those of thunderstorms or an animal that may behave unpredictably. And some phobias, such as that of flying, are tricky to break down into equally sized steps. In such cases imaginary or virtual exposure may be used instead. The use of virtual reality has been shown to be effective for fear of flying. Clinical psychologist Lars-Göran Öst developed a single session treatment for phobias whereby the patient and therapist attempt to work up the patient's hierarchy in a single session (usually a half day). This has practical advantages (e.g. not having to keep spiders for many weeks) and Öst found that '90% of the patients were much improved or completely recovered after a mean of 2.1 hours of therapy.' In some instances psychologists have collaborated with commercial airlines to offer exposure-based fear-of-flying courses.

The principles of classical conditioning have been utilized across situations ranging from advertising for cars and alcohol to protecting endangered species or livestock. To stop lions from preying on cattle they are given beef laced with chemicals that induce nausea. This will result in the lions developing a food aversion to beef as they associate it with an unpleasant response (nausea). Similarly, advertising for cars or alcohol frequently involves beautiful models. Research has shown that men who viewed a car advertisement that included a beautiful woman later rated the car as being faster, more appealing, and better designed than men who viewed the advertisement for the same car without the beautiful woman. Similarly advertising agencies are very quick to cancel contracts with celebrities who have been disgraced, as they are no longer associated with positive connotations or emotions.

Operant conditioning

Some psychologists, such as Burrhus Frederic Skinner viewed classical conditioning as too simplistic to be a complete explanation of all learning. The result was the development of the theory of *operant conditioning*, also known as *instrumental conditioning or instrumental learning*. This theory of learning was based on Edward Thorndike's 1927 *Law of Effect* which he proposed after observations of cats trying to escape from a puzzle box. In order to escape, the cat had to press a lever. He discovered that with repeated trials, a cat would escape more quickly, as ineffective attempts were made less frequently, and effective attempts were made more frequently. Eventually the cat would go straight to the lever. So the cat learnt how to get out of the box. This is an example of operant conditioning, a mode of learning in which the strength or frequency of a behaviour is influenced by its consequences, such as reward or punishment, and the behaviour is controlled by antecedents called *discriminative stimuli*, which come to signal those consequences. Thorndike's Law of Effect states that responses that produce a satisfying effect (or escape from a discomfort) in a particular situation become more likely to occur again in that situation, and responses that have the effect of producing discomfort become less likely to occur again in that situation. In short, some consequences strengthen behaviour and other consequences weaken behaviour. Skinner identified two types of operant that affect behaviour:

- *Reinforcers*: responses from the environment that increase the likelihood of the behaviour being repeated.
- *Punishers*: responses from the environment that decrease the likelihood of the behaviour being repeated.

Skinner used an operant conditioning chamber, known as a 'Skinner Box', to show how positive and negative punishment and reinforcement worked. A Skinner box is a puzzle box in which animals such as pigeons or rats could be exposed to carefully controlled stimuli. The box contained a lever that dispensed food if the animal pressed it. As the animal moved about the box it would eventually press the lever by chance and the animals quickly learned to press the lever to obtain food, demonstrating positive reinforcement of lever pressing behaviour. Skinner demonstrated negative reinforcement by subjecting the animal to an unpleasant electric current which could be switched off by pressing a lever (*escape learning*). Again, over repeated trials the animals learnt to press the lever straight away. The consequence of escaping the electric current ensured that they would repeat the action. Indeed, when a light preceded the electric current being switched on, the animals would learn to press the lever to prevent the current being switched on (*avoidance learning*). When the reinforcement involves adding something (such as food) to a situation to increase the probability of the behaviour (lever pressing) it is called *positive reinforcement*. Negative reinforcement is when something is taken away (the aversive electric current) to increase the probability of the behaviour. Some stimuli that act as reinforcers are inherently rewarding (*primary reinforcers*) because they satisfy a need, such as for food or water. In contrast *secondary reinforcers* are things that are only rewarding because they are associated with a primary reinforcer. For example, money is a secondary reinforcer as it can be used to buy things that satisfy needs (primary reinforcers).

Punishment is the opposite of reinforcement in that it acts to weaken or decrease the strength or frequency of a response, and punishment can be positive or negative too. *Positive punishment* is when you add an aversive stimulus to reduce the frequency of a behaviour. For example, reprimanding a child for being naughty. In contrast, *negative punishment* is when something pleasant is removed as in 'time out' to discourage undesirable behaviour. Despite these conceptual differences, in practice it can be difficult to differentiate the two—if a child gets a detention for talking in class, is the punishment positive or negative? It is positive because an unpleasant stimulus (the detention) has been added, but also negative because access to a pleasant stimulus has been removed (whatever the child would have been doing without the detention). In general, it is more effective to try to reinforce desirable behaviour than to punish undesirable behaviour. However, this can be challenging as often on a practical level what we most want is to reduce the frequency of undesirable behaviour (e.g. aggression), and it can be difficult to work out how to effectively reward its absence, especially if it is a low frequency behaviour. Furthermore, there is some evidence that providing external rewards can undermine intrinsic motivation. So rewarding a child for eating vegetables may in fact decrease their liking of vegetables, even if it increases their eating of them. (See Table 1.)

The rate at which the reward is given also affects how powerful it is as a reinforcer. The power of the reinforcement is measured in two ways. First, the *response rate*, which is the frequency of the behaviour, that is, how many times the rat presses the lever; and, second, *the extinction rate*, which is how long it takes the rat to stop pressing the lever once food is discontinued.

The delivery of reinforcement according to a specific schedule or rule is known as a *reinforcement schedule*, and the main types are shown in Table 2. As you can see from Table 2, paradoxically it is

Table 1. Types of punishment and reinforcement

	Positive (adds a stimuli)	Negative (removes a stimuli)
Reinforcement (increases likelihood of behaviour being repeated)	Example: Rewarding children for good school attendance with money.	Example: Fining parents whose children do not have good attendance.
Punishment (decreases likelihood of behaviour being repeated)	Example: Having to write lines for talking in class.	Example: Being kept in at break time for talking in class.

Table 2. Schedules of reinforcement

Reinforcement schedule	Reward	Response rate	Extinction rate
Continuous	Reward every time the behaviour is exhibited (e.g. patient-controlled doses of pain medication).	Low—there is no need to work especially hard as you can get the reward whenever you want it.	Fast—it is quickly clear that the action no longer produces the reward.
Fixed interval	Reward after a fixed time length providing the behaviour has been exhibited at least once in that time (e.g. timed doses of pain medication).	Medium—there is some motivation to work for the reward.	Medium—it is worth continuing to try for a while to see if it is going to start working again like it has done before.
Fixed ratio	Reward after the behaviour occurs a specified number of times (e.g. a treat when a child earns five stars on their chart).	Response rate is high as more work directly leads to more reward.	Extinction rate is medium as it takes a while to work out that the rules have changed.
Variable ratio	Behaviour is rewarded after an unpredictable number of times (e.g. buying lottery ticket or gambling).	Response rate is high as you don't know how much work you need to do to earn the reward.	Extinction rate is slow because it is difficult to know that the reward is no longer available if it was always unpredictable.
Variable interval	Reward after a variable time length providing the behaviour has been exhibited at least once in that time (e.g. checking your emails).	Response rate is high as you don't know how much work you need to do to earn the reward.	Extinction rate is slow because it is difficult to know that the reward is no longer available if it was always unpredictable.

not the case that the more reliably you get a reward, the more strongly you exhibit the behaviour. The strongest reinforcers are often those that are least predictable, which may help to explain the lure of gambling or buying lottery tickets.

The principles of operant conditioning have been used to influence behaviour in many settings. Such interventions are often some form of *behaviour modification programme* which utilizes schedules of reinforcement and/or punishment in order to increase the frequency of desired behaviours and/or decrease the frequency of undesirable behaviours. This is common in classroom settings where praise or rewards are given for good work and behaviour, and punishments for poor work or behaviour. Research shows that rewarding inputs is more effective than rewarding outputs—so rewarding children with money for studying (inputs) leads to better test scores than rewarding them directly for better test scores (outputs). Such research suggests that 'pay-for-performance' schemes for teachers, where they are remunerated based on their students' test scores (outputs), may not be the most effective strategy.

The principles of operant conditioning are often used in child behaviour management with star charts and rewards for good behaviour and timeout on 'the naughty step' for undesirable behaviour. Similar interventions have been employed to enhance school attendance, for example by rewarding good attendance with money or vouchers, or by fining parents for a child's poor school attendance. An entire organization may employ such a strategy. Some psychiatric hospitals or educational facilities use a system called a *token economy* whereby tokens are earned for desired behaviour and can be exchanged for rewards such as snacks or access to specific privileges or activities. Prisons are also often based on such principles with rewards such television privileges for good behaviour, or the absence of bad behaviour, and punishments such as isolation for unwanted behaviour. Indeed, it could be argued that a society based on the use of money is one large token economy whereby desired behaviour (work) is rewarded with tokens (money) which gives access to rewards.

This chapter has covered the first two forms of learning—classical and operant conditioning. The third form, observational learning, is thought to involve more cognitive mediation, and that is what we move on to look at in Chapter 2.

Chapter 2
Putting the 'C' into CBT

The study of classical and operant conditioning led to great advances in understanding learning, but these theories don't consider any individual factors, such as the role of genetic or cognitive factors in learning—in other words, they don't explain individual variation in learning in a shared environment. Furthermore, they cannot explain all forms of learning. For example, German psychologist Wolfgang Köhler observed that chimps trying to access a banana that was out of reach sometimes seemed to find the solution (stacking up boxes or using a tool to reach the banana) in a flash of insight rather than solely by trial and error (Figure 2). Insight learning is what happens when you suddenly 'see' the solution to a problem even when you are not actively trying to solve it.

Similarly, American psychologist Edward Tolman found evidence of *latent learning* in rats by showing that they could learn their way around a maze in the absence of any reward, and then use this knowledge to find the reward more quickly once it was available. The rats had developed a *cognitive map* of the maze despite there being no external reward for doing so at that time. And *social learning theory*, developed by the American psychologist, Albert Bandura, suggests that humans can learn via observation rather than solely through personal experience. Bandura noted that behaviour could be learned from the

2. Chimpanzees problem solving to access a banana.

environment through observation or instruction, and that cognitive processes mediated this learning and the associations between stimuli and responses. In addition to learning by observing behaviour, learning is also influenced by observing behaviour being rewarded or punished, a process known as *vicarious reinforcement*—seeing someone else being punished for an act puts us off doing it. For example, public hangings were thought to act as a deterrent to others.

Social learning theory

In the early 1960s, Bandura carried out a series of studies in which children watched adults interacting with an inflatable, weighted doll (called a Bobo doll) which bounces up when pushed down. Children who observed an adult interacting with the doll in an aggressive manner, by shouting at it and punching it, were much more likely to behave aggressively to the doll than children who had observed an adult interacting with the doll in a non-aggressive manner. This was especially so when the adult was seen being praised rather than reprimanded for their aggressive behaviour. The fact that observational learning is influenced by seeing the consequences of the behaviour suggests a cognitive component to learning. The effect was even stronger when the adult was the same gender as the child observing. This is because we *identify* with models (individuals that we observe are referred to as models) that we perceive to be more similar to ourselves, and models that we perceive to have been rewarded. Such models are not just the actors used in experiments but form part of our sociocultural context and thus everyone around us including friends, family, teachers, co-workers, and people in the media. These models provide examples of behaviour to observe and imitate, e.g. masculine or feminine ideals, pro- and anti-social behaviour, etc. Social media provides a plethora of potential models, as well as clear indications of their popularity or status. The process of observational learning may help to explain why suicide rates go up in the wake of a celebrity, or even a fictional character on television, committing suicide. The role of violence on television or in computer games in promoting aggressive behaviour has been hotly debated, with no clear conclusion.

The different theories of learning are not mutually exclusive, and it may be that the most potent learning occurs when they are combined. For example, children are learning by observation when they *imitate* what adult role models do, so children of smokers are more likely to smoke. However, the sociocultural context, and consequently operant conditioning, will also have an effect—if the smoking behaviour is rewarded by social approval from peers it is more likely to continue than if it is met with disapproval or other negative consequences. As well as being positive or negative, reinforcement can be external or internal. If an individual gets approval from others, this approval is an *external reinforcer*, but feeling happy about being approved of is an *internal reinforcer*. Alternatively, it may be disapproval from others that is the reward, as in rebellious behaviour. The fact that what is rewarding for one person, or in one situation, is different for another person or situation highlights the role of cognitive mediation in the learning process.

Cognitive revolution

The detailed study of antecedents, behaviours, and consequences by learning theorists prompted therapists to use a similar approach, known as functional analysis, to understand their patients' difficulties. *Functional analysis* is the process of examining in detail the antecedents to or triggers for the behaviour, the behaviour itself, and the consequences of the behaviour. The purpose of functional analysis is to understand why behaviour that is unhelpful or distressing, persists. This, along with learning theories, was used to develop useful treatments such as systematic desensitization or graduated exposure therapy for phobias. However, these interventions still focused primarily on the observable phenomena of behaviour and its consequences. By the 1970s, the disregard of all unobservable psychological processes, particularly the role of thought in influencing human behaviour and emotion, was causing increasing dissatisfaction. Several strands of work sought to bring cognitive phenomena into the understanding of psychological disorders, and this development became known as the *cognitive revolution*.

One of the pioneers in this area was American psychologist Albert Ellis. Although originally trained in classical psychoanalysis, Ellis, like many others, became frustrated by its limitations. Ellis had had a difficult childhood himself and dealt with this by taking a pragmatic approach to the challenges and realizing that he could cope with significant adversity by learning to mind it less. These experiences are likely to have laid the foundations for his development of a new form of therapy which he called *Rational Therapy*, and subsequently expanded into *Rational Emotive Behaviour Therapy* (REBT). REBT is a scientific approach that continues to evolve, but it is based on the ABC model shown in Figure 3 where the 'B' of beliefs mediates the relationship between the A of antecedent and C of consequences. So the antecedent may be a loss, and an irrational belief that the loss should not have occurred and is intolerable leads to the consequence of emotional distress. However, if the belief was a more rational one (e.g. I am sad that the loss has occurred, but it is tolerable) then the emotional consequences will be lessened.

REBT implies that if we want to change dysfunctional psychological outcomes, such as anxiety and depression, then we must change the underlying irrational beliefs. Ellis viewed irrational beliefs as often taking the form of extreme or dogmatic 'musts', 'shoulds', or 'oughts', in contrast to more rational and flexible desires, wishes, or preferences. So rather than thinking 'I must be the best at everything' a more flexible, rational belief would be 'although it is nice to do well at things, it isn't possible to be the best at everything all the time'. REBT strategies focus on

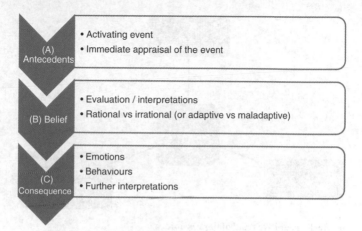

(A) Antecedents	• Activating event • Immediate appraisal of the event
(B) Belief	• Evaluation / interpretations • Rational vs irrational (or adaptive vs maladaptive)
(C) Consequence	• Emotions • Behaviours • Further interpretations

3. ABC Model (functional analysis).

changing patients' self-defeating beliefs and behaviours by demonstrating their irrationality and rigidity. Ellis believed that through the rational analysis and re-evaluation of such beliefs, patients would understand the self-defeatingness of their irrational beliefs and then could develop more rational alternatives. Ellis's work was quite controversial at the time, particularly as his own therapeutic style could be confrontational and involved humour. For example, to discourage patients from having rigid, overly demanding beliefs, such as believing that they *must* feel or behave in a certain way, he would accuse them of 'musterbating'. Or of 'awfulizing' when they were overly focused on the negative aspects of a situation. It is reported that in order to overcome his own fear of speaking to women he forced himself to speak to over a hundred women in a local park. In 1959, Ellis founded the Institute for Rational Living (now called the Albert Ellis Institute) to further study and training in REBT, and he was a prolific writer who authored and co-authored more than eighty books.

Around the same time as Ellis was developing REBT, the American psychiatrist Aaron T. Beck (1921–2021), who was similarly

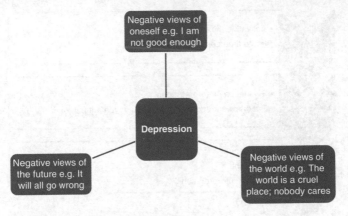

4. Beck's cognitive triad of depression.

disillusioned with the Freudian psychoanalytic approach, began developing his own hypotheses about the role of thoughts (also known as cognitions) in psychological disorders. Beck noticed that his depressed patients seemed to spontaneously experience streams of negative thoughts. He termed these *negative automatic thoughts* and noticed that they tended to occur in three related domains: the *cognitive triad* of negative thoughts about the self, others, and future.

Beck began trying to help patients identify and evaluate their negative automatic thoughts and found that by doing so, patients were able to think more realistically, which led them to feel better emotionally and behave in more helpful ways. This observation led him to propose the cognitive theory of depression in 1979, which was later extended to other areas of emotional disorder (Figure 4). Research trials showing that Beck's cognitive therapy was effective in reducing depression strengthened the approach, and further evolution and amalgamation of cognitive and behavioural approaches led to the development of modern CBT, which is described in more detail in the coming chapters.

Chapter 3
The theory behind CBT

In Hamlet, Shakespeare writes 'There is nothing either good or bad, but thinking makes it so', recognizing that the way in which we interpret events influences our emotional reactions to them. The fundamental idea behind CBT is that how you perceive a situation influences how you feel in that situation. For example, being ignored by an acquaintance will provoke a different emotional reaction depending on how you interpret it. The emotional response might be anxiety ('Maybe I've done something to upset her?'); depression ('Nobody would want to speak to me anyway, I'm too dull'); or anger ('She's got a nerve being so snooty—I don't deserve such a snub!'). On the other hand, the reaction might be neutral ('She's probably distracted and hasn't noticed me').

According to the classic text by Beck and colleagues in 1979, CBT is 'an active, directive, structured approach, based on an underlying theoretical rationale that an individual's affect and behaviour are largely determined by the way in which he structures the world'. The fundamental idea is that thoughts and feelings will affect, and be affected by, your behaviour and physiological reactions. And all of this is influenced by the environment around you. So, it is not just what happens to you that determines your emotional experience but also your interpretation of what has happened. When an emotion seems out of proportion to the event, the individual's idiosyncratic meaning attached to the event can explain the emotional reaction. So to understand people's distress we must understand their 'meanings', that is their cognitions, their individual way of perceiving their experiences in the world. This opens up the possibility of being able to reduce their distress by helping them to modify these interpretations.

Formulation

All forms of psychotherapy utilize *formulation*—that is, a theoretical understanding of how emotional problems develop and are maintained. Formulation is one of the most fundamental ways in which the various schools of psychotherapy differ. Formulation in CBT is differentiated from other schools of psychotherapy not only by the theories it draws upon but also by the way in which it is approached. Formulation in CBT is collaborative and transparent, and it is hypothesis driven. The formulation, the understanding of the patient's difficulties, is devised collaboratively between the patient and the therapist. The therapist brings expertise of cognitive and behavioural theories, but the patient is the expert on their own experience. Together the patient and therapist develop hypotheses about what might have led to the development of the problem(s), and what keeps the problem(s) going.

An initial formulation is proposed as a hypothesis, or collection of hypotheses, to be further developed, tested, and refined throughout therapy. A CBT formulation should be *idiosyncratic*, in that it is personalized to that individual. Elements of the formulation will be common to other people with similar problems or experiences, but the exact content of a CBT formulation will reflect only that one person's experience. To be useful the formulation should explain not only the development of the problem but also what keeps it going in the here and now. It is these maintenance factors, that keep the problem going, that give rise to the targets for treatment, i.e. what needs to change for that person not to have the problem anymore.

Beck's theory of emotional disorders

Given CBT's focus on cognition, on the individual's interpretation of events, the CBT model needs to explain how people come to make such characteristic interpretations. Beck outlined his theory of how emotional disorders develop in his 1976 book *Cognitive Therapy and the Emotional Disorders*. He suggested that, based on formative early experiences, people develop *core beliefs* (also sometimes called *basic beliefs* or *unconditional beliefs*) about themselves, the world, and other people. If these core beliefs are negative (e.g., 'I'm not good enough' or 'the world is a bad place') then the individual must find a way of coping in spite of them. For example, they must find ways of managing life's challenges given their belief that they are not as good or as capable as they perceive themselves to need to be. So they develop rules to help them to manage in spite of their negative core beliefs. Some of these rules may be dysfunctional and are called *dysfunctional assumptions* (also sometimes called *conditional beliefs* or *rules for living*). These 'if, then' rules guide our behaviour and help us to cope in the face of negative core beliefs about ourselves, others, or the world. Such rules may have been functional (adaptive) in the circumstances in which they were learnt, but may be less adaptive in subsequent circumstances and hence can trigger emotional disorder. For example, a rule such as 'I must keep others at a distance or they will try to control me' could have been an adaptive response to enmeshed family relationships, but outside of that social context, it is likely to have significant disadvantages such as isolation.

The final type of belief (or thought) seen as important in the CBT model of emotional disorder is *automatic thoughts*. These are the more surface level thoughts that are specific to the current situation, and are believed to have more of a role in maintaining,

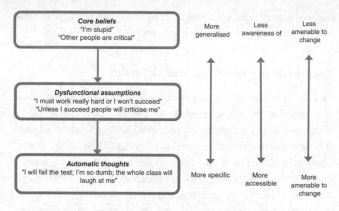

5. Characteristics of the different 'levels' of cognition.

rather than causing, emotional disorders. So Beck's model sets out three different levels or types of cognition that are thought to be important—*core beliefs*, *dysfunctional assumptions*, and *automatic thoughts*—and the characteristics of these types or levels of cognitions is outlined in Figure 5.

At the most accessible, surface level are *automatic thoughts* which are the stream of consciousness that runs through our mind. Like the hum of the fridge or background road noise, we may not always be paying attention to them, but we can choose to tune into them if we want to. They are the most specific, least generalized type of thought. At the opposite end of the continuum are *core beliefs* which are less accessible and more generalized. Core beliefs are absolute, unconditional beliefs about ourselves, others, or the world. Negative core beliefs include things like 'I'm stupid' or 'other people are untrustworthy', and these beliefs then act as a filter on our experience, causing us to notice and remember information that is consistent with them. The *dysfunctional assumptions* are at a level in between automatic thoughts and core beliefs, and are the rules we use to guide our behaviour. Dysfunctional assumptions usually concern what people believe

Examples of more and less adaptive assumptions

Achievement

'If I can't do it perfectly there's no point in trying' vs 'It's nice to do well but it's unrealistic to expect to do everything perfectly'

Acceptance

'If someone doesn't like me it means there's something wrong with me' vs 'I don't need everyone's approval in order to feel good about myself'

Control

'Asking for help is a sign of weakness' vs 'Asking for help can be a way of finding a solution and is better than unnecessary struggling alone'.

they need to be happy or safe, how they should behave in order to see themselves as worthwhile, and what standards they expect from themselves, others, and the world in general. The major concerns centre around acceptance, achievement, and control. The box gives examples of more and less functional assumptions in these domains.

For example, someone who, based on early experiences such as struggling at school, forms the core belief 'I'm stupid' will develop rules or strategies to get by despite believing themselves to be stupid. They may work extremely hard to compensate for their perceived stupidity and thus may in fact do very well. This would reflect the assumption 'I must try harder than others to keep up' and may be adaptive in many situations. Alternatively, they may do the opposite and not try at all, in order to avoid being exposed as stupid, or because they are so convinced that they will fail that they cannot see any point in trying. This would likely be a less adaptive strategy. The situations in which they find themselves will also have an influence. If the person who uses the strategy of always working hard to compensate encounters a situation in which they are unable put in extra effort, or fail to meet the desired standard in spite of working hard, then their belief that they are stupid will be triggered and they will become more aware of it, which will be liable to lead to distress. Someone who does not have the core belief that they are stupid may attribute such failures to circumstances or bad luck, and thus be less distressed by the experience, and potentially more likely to try again.

Beliefs and assumptions may be dysfunctional because of their content—anyone who believes 'I am bad' is likely to suffer—but their content may not be as clearly dysfunctional. For example, independence is valued in some sociocultural contexts and there may be advantages to not relying on others, depending on what context you are in. Core beliefs and dysfunctional assumptions tend to be overly rigid and/or extreme, and not reflect the complexity of human nature. Of course it is nice to prioritize the needs of others, when you have the resources to do so, but to feel compelled to always put others first is unlikely to be adaptive in many situations.

Both core beliefs and dysfunctional assumptions are thought to predispose the individual to emotional disorder, depending on the circumstances. Automatic thoughts have more of a role in maintaining the disorder once it has been triggered. All three types interact with each other, as well as with physiological and behavioural responses, to keep an individual 'stuck'. Although Beck's work originally focused on depression, his *cognitive model of emotional disorder* has been applied across the range of emotional disorders, and the version of the model shown in Figure 6 below is a generic amalgamation of different versions that can be used to attempt to understand the development of any emotional problem and the maintaining cycles that keep them going. We will consider next how cognitive behavioural theories understand how psychological problems develop and are

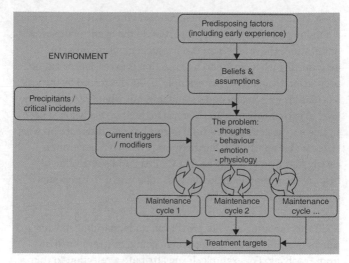

6. Generic CBT model.

maintained, before going on to look at the interventions used to tackle them.

Implications of the CBT model

As we have seen, a basic premise of the CBT model is that it is not solely events themselves that matter, but the way that we interpret them. Thus, in order to help people, we need to understand their thought processes, that is, their typical and situation-specific ways of perceiving the world. The same event can have quite different meanings, as described above in the example of being ignored by an acquaintance. However, this depends on the context—there are some events that are universally distressing, such as the experience of trauma or the loss of loved ones, and a criticism of CBT is that its emphasis on the individual's interpretation of events has the potential to invalidate the individual's distress in response to difficult life circumstances. If you are diagnosed with a life-threatening illness, no amount of CBT will make that good news. Where CBT has the potential to add most value is where an emotional reaction is out of proportion to the event in its severity or duration. However, there is some judgement involved in determining when an emotional reaction is excessive, or out of proportion to an event. For example, being distressed by the loss of a child is universally understandable, but what about the same level of extreme distress in response to the loss of a beloved pet? In this way societal and cultural norms have an influence on what is deemed proportional. Furthermore, even when an event is clearly distressing, it may be that CBT can add some value in helping the person to make the best adjustment to the changed circumstances.

A CBT formulation aims to provide an understanding of what causes the difficulties, or keeps them going, or prevents them from resolving. For example, if you attribute a rejection to your inherent unlovability, then this will influence your emotional and behavioural responses differently than if you attributed the rejection to circumstances or bad luck. Attributing rejection to a fault in yourself is likely to lead to greater distress and will likely influence your future behaviour in situations where rejection is a possibility—for example, by avoiding relationships, trying too hard to please, or pretending to be someone that you are not. These responses in turn may influence the likelihood of further rejection as shown in Figure 7. This is just one example of the type of maintenance cycle that could be incorporated into an idiosyncratic version of the generic model shown in Figure 6.

The importance of experience and sociocultural context

Because CBT focuses on the present, on the hypothesized maintaining cycles, it is often criticized for ignoring the individual's previous experience (history) and the broader sociocultural context. However, this is not necessarily the case. The generic CBT model shown in Figure 6 suggests that

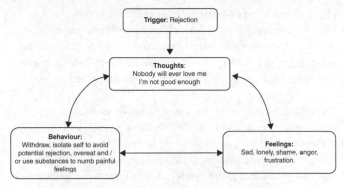

7. Vicious cycle showing how rejection might be responded to.

predisposing factors, including previous experience, make you vulnerable to emotional disorder, that your thoughts (at all three levels) have an important role in maintaining the problem, and that all of this occurs in the context of your environment. CBT therapist David Westbrook, a former director of the Oxford Cognitive Therapy Centre, used the analogy of a fire to explain CBT's focus on maintenance factors—if you discover a fire you don't start to tackle it by looking for the match that lit the fire—you start by addressing the factors that are keeping it going in the here and now—the supply of fuel and oxygen. However, once the current crisis is under control, it may be worth investigating what caused the fire, or increased the risk of it happening in the first place, in order to reduce the risk of it happening again. The process is similar in CBT—the initial focus is on identifying and addressing what is keeping the problem going in the here and now, the relevant thoughts, feelings, behaviours, and physiology. But once those factors have been addressed, it is worth exploring the vulnerability factors such as core beliefs and dysfunctional assumptions to see if those factors can be modified such that the person is less vulnerable to the problem recurring in the future. And the sociocultural context may be very relevant to those vulnerability factors in influencing the rules that we internalize about how to live. For example, rates of eating disorders are highest in industrialized cultures where there is an emphasis on thinness, particularly if thinness is linked to success. This can be especially so in professions or sports where a certain body type is desirable (e.g, ballet, jockeying, gymnastics, modelling, acting).

The CBT model suggests that, on the basis of formative experiences, you develop core beliefs about yourself and the world. If these formative experiences are negative, then you are more likely to develop negative core beliefs. Hence, adverse childhood experiences, such as abuse, neglect, bereavement, or significant household dysfunction, have been consistently linked to depression, anxiety, and even suicide, in adulthood. Interestingly, such adverse childhood experiences have also been shown to predict poorer outcomes across non-psychological domains such as teenage pregnancy and physical health conditions such as asthma. The method by which such experiences lead to poorer health outcomes is not fully understood and is likely to be via multiple pathways. Clearly there is a direct impact of poverty and social determinants of health such as employment and income, and of increased use of health harming behaviours such as smoking, poor diet, and substance use. However, recent research suggests that there may be broader impacts of adverse childhood experience such as changing the responses of the pleasure and reward centres in the brain, with brain imaging studies showing differences in specific brain areas (e.g. the prefrontal cortex and amygdala) between those who have and those who haven't had adverse experiences in childhood, and showing that the impact of adverse experiences is cumulative with a greater number of adverse experiences having a bigger the impact. This research suggests that children who have experienced adversity are more likely to overreact to stressors as adults.

While CBT acknowledges the role of the predisposing factors such as adverse childhood experiences, genetics, and brain chemistry, it views these factors as less amenable to change and instead concentrates on the beliefs and behavioural or emotional response patterns that have developed as a result of these experiences. Experiences, whether adverse of not, will teach us rules about the world, ourselves, and other people. Such rules, according to Bob Schwartz,

> come from our experience, some event or events in our life that have caused us to make a decision about ourselves, about how to operate in life, about how to succeed or how to survive. Personal laws have their purpose, but when they become unconscious and start operating automatically, we're stuck with them long after they've stopped playing a useful function. Even worse, many of the most powerful personal laws were made when we were too young to have an accurate picture of who we are or of what the world is actually like, and so are often terribly misguided.

Schwartz's quote, from an unrelated book about dieting, highlights why early experience can have such a pivotal effect—the earlier the experience occurs, the more likely it is to be interpreted in immature black and white ways—as 'good' or 'bad'—and the less able it is to take account of context, or balance competing viewpoints, leading to absolute beliefs.

As we have seen, the individual then develops strategies to get by in spite of their negative core beliefs. These rules, personal laws, or in CBT language, 'assumptions', may be more or less functional. Indeed, they may have been highly functional in the circumstance in which they were learnt but may become dysfunctional in other situations. For example, the abused child may develop the assumption 'I must not let my feelings show' as an effective and necessary way of coping with a volatile parent. However, as an adult there will be significant disadvantages to never expressing feelings, and this may put the person at risk of emotional disorder.

Figure 8 shows an example of a patient whose assumptions lay dormant until they were activated by environmental events. Neil

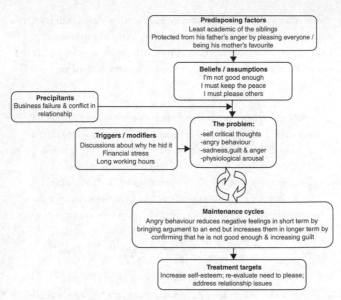

Predisposing factors
Least academic of the siblings
Protected from his father's anger by pleasing everyone /
being his mother's favourite

Beliefs / assumptions
I'm not good enough
I must keep the peace
I must please others

Precipitants
Business failure & conflict in
relationship

Triggers / modifiers
Discussions about why he hid it
Financial stress
Long working hours

The problem:
-self critical thoughts
-angry behaviour
-sadness, guilt & anger
-physiological arousal

Maintenance cycles
Angry behaviour reduces negative feelings in short term by
bringing argument to an end but increases them in longer term by
confirming that he is not good enough & increasing guilt

Treatment targets
Increase self-esteem; re-evaluate need to please;
address relationship issues

8. **Diagrammatic formulation of Neil's difficulties.**

(names and identifying details have been changed to protect confidentiality) did not become depressed until his mid-60s, despite having formed the relevant underlying beliefs in childhood. Neil was referred for CBT because of low mood (depression) and angry outbursts. He had not suffered from depression or excessive anger previously, and his current difficulties had been triggered by the failure of a business that he ran with his wife. As the business began to experience financial difficulties Neil believed that he would be able to overcome the difficulties in time, so he worked even harder and hid the extent of the difficulties from his wife in order to protect her from the stress. But the financial difficulties got progressively worse, until Neil was left with no choice but to close the business and reveal the extent of the debts to his wife. The closing of the business and change to their financial situation meant Neil and his wife had to delay their retirement plans and take jobs that they would not otherwise have taken. It also caused conflict in their relationship—Neil's wife was particularly upset that he had concealed the extent of the difficulties from her and questioned what else he may be keeping from her. It was during these arguments that Neil experienced overwhelming anger and responded by storming off or throwing things. Such behaviour brought the argument to an end but did little to resolve the relationship issues and caused him to feel even worse about himself. The current context was also relevant in that a different partner may have had less trouble in adjusting to the changed circumstances or may have been more understanding of why he had concealed the difficulties. Figure 8 shows a diagrammatic formulation of Neil's difficulties.

Neil's formulation shows how beliefs formed in childhood made him vulnerable to psychological distress in later life. However, this was not activated until triggering environmental circumstances arose. Previously this vulnerability had not caused any difficulties as he had managed to live within the constraints of his beliefs—he had been able to please others and keep the peace well enough until a particularly challenging set of circumstances arose. Then he got stuck in maintenance cycles whereby what he did in the short term to manage the situation actually exacerbated the problem in the longer term—his aggressive behaviour then brought arguments to an end but made him feel even worse about himself in the long run.

What keeps the problems going?

The generic CBT model shown in Figure 6 includes both development (what caused the problem) and maintenance (what keeps it going) factors. As regards maintenance, the model identifies four key elements—thoughts, feelings, behaviours, and physiology. These four elements also interact with the environment, which includes the individual's social and cultural context. The effect of the environment is reciprocal—the individual is affected by their environment, but they also have an

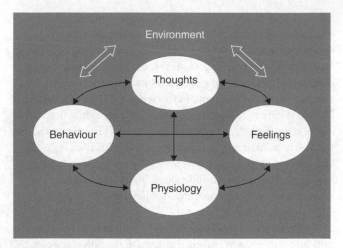

9. Hot cross bun style of formulation.

impact on the environment. For example, being in a hostile environment will affect how the individual responds, thinks, feels, and behaves—perceiving your surroundings to be hostile may make you more likely to react in hostile or aggressive ways, which in turn will impact on those around you. These elements are depicted in Figure 9 in the form of a 'hot cross bun' (named after the round bun marked with a cross on the top, traditionally eaten on Good Friday) shown below. This type of formulation is also known as the '5-systems' or '5 areas approach', with the fifth area being the influence of the environment.

The hot cross bun style of formulation has the advantage of being simple and easy to understand. It lists the four main elements of the problem and places them in the context of the individual and their environment, while recognizing the interacting relationships between the different components. However, what it fails to do is to draw out the specific maintaining cycles—in this type of formulation everything is seen as leading to everything, and vice versa. When we examine Neil's formulation we can see that this is

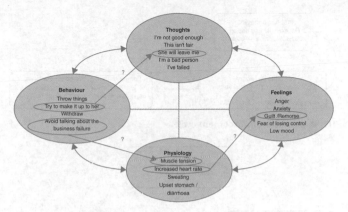

10. Problems with hot cross bun formulation of Neil's difficulties.

not the case—not all thoughts, feelings, behaviours, and physiological sensations link to each other equally (Figure 10). It is the throwing things rather than the trying to make it up to his wife that leads him to think that she might leave him. Similarly, increased heart rate is not a source of his guilt or remorse.

The purpose of the formulation in CBT is not only to explain how the problem developed but to examine the relationships between important components in order to understand what keeps it going. It is specifying these relationships that enables CBT therapists to work out what needs to change for the person not to have the problem anymore. So the most useful type of CBT formulation will include all the elements shown in Figure 9 but will go further in that it will organize the main components of the problem (thoughts, feelings, behaviour, and physiology) into *maintaining cycles*. Maintaining cycles, sometimes called *vicious cycles*, specify the functional relationships between the elements that serve to keep the problem going. Often it is the case that what the individual is doing in an attempt to solve the problem is inadvertently maintaining the problem. For example, what Neil was doing in the short term inadvertently maintained the problem in the longer term, as shown in Figure 11.

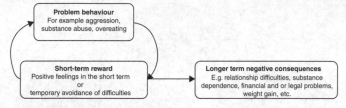

11. Short-term reinforcement cycle.

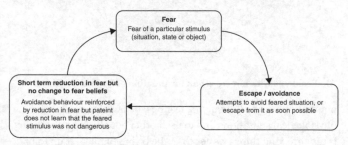

12. How avoidance maintains fear.

Avoidance can work in a similar way—by avoiding the stimuli that make them anxious, the individual feels better in the short term, but it maintains their anxiety, as they never get to find out that the thing that they were anxious about wasn't actually dangerous, or at least not as dangerous as they had feared it would be (Figure 12).

The figures below give further examples of typical maintaining cycles that keep people 'stuck' in their current patterns of thinking, feeling, and behaving. Figure 13 depicts a common maintaining cycle in anxiety whereby the anxiety symptoms themselves are perceived as a threat, leading to an escalation of anxiety and an increased perception of threat, and further escalating anxiety. This is one of the ways in which physiology drives changes in thoughts, feelings, and behaviour.

Figures 14 and 15 show maintaining cycles that are more typical in depression than anxiety as they act to lower mood.

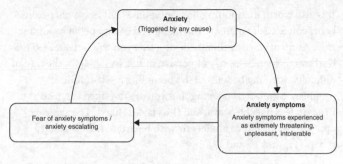

13. Fear of fear as a maintaining cycle.

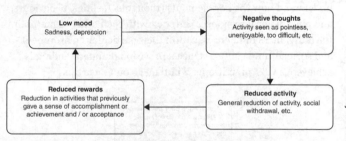

14. Reduced activity and rewards maintain low mood.

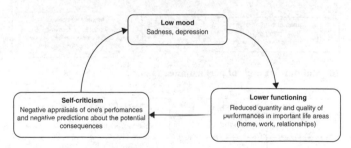

15. Self-criticism maintains low mood.

It is also worth mentioning how sometimes holding a particular belief can actually increase the likelihood of that belief becoming true. As mentioned earlier, believing that you will not succeed may lead you to try less hard, not persist, or not seek help in the face of difficulty, with the belief thereby becoming a self-fulfilling prophecy. Similarly, believing that you are not liked can lead you to act in less likeable ways, and thus be less liked. The same can apply to performance anxiety or with regard to beliefs about others (Figures 16 and 17).

To conclude, the purpose of a CBT formulation is to try to understand how the key elements (thoughts, feelings, behaviours, and physiological responses) interact with each other to maintain the individual's difficulties, within their particular environment and sociocultural context. Once a provisional understanding is achieved, a CBT practitioner will then go on to use this

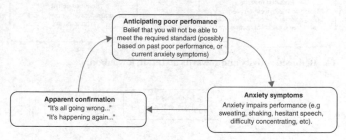

16. **Maintaining cycle of performance anxiety.**

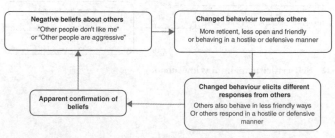

17. **Self-fulfilling prophecy maintaining cycle.**

understanding to decide where to intervene—to decide what needs to change for the person not to be 'stuck' in the vicious cycles that maintain their problems. Before we look at the methods that CBT uses to do this, we will first consider the way in which CBT goes about it, its style and structure, which form the backdrop against which CBT methods are implemented.

Chapter 4
The style and structure of CBT

Like all therapies, CBT has its own style. Compared to other forms of psychotherapy, CBT is usually more problem focused, structured, and brief. However, many elements of CBT's style and structure are common to most forms of therapy. For example, weekly meetings of an hour's duration. Similarly, most psychological therapies recognize the importance of having a good relationship between the patient and therapist—the *therapeutic relationship* or *therapeutic alliance*. The American psychologist Carl Rogers highlighted the importance of the *core conditions* of empathy, genuineness, and unconditional positive regard in forming effective therapeutic relationships. While some therapeutic approaches view the therapeutic relationship as the primary mechanism of change, CBT views it as necessary but not sufficient for change to be achieved. That is, without a good therapeutic relationship it is unlikely that positive change will be achieved, but a good therapeutic relationship alone will not inevitably produce therapeutic change. The theoretical basis underpinning CBT is, after all, that change is achieved by breaking the maintaining cycles of thoughts, feelings, physiology, and behaviour hypothesized to be keeping the problem(s) going. This chapter gives an overview of the main elements of CBT's style and how they are used. For a more detailed comparison of CBT with other psychotherapeutic approaches, see *Psychotherapy: A Very Short Introduction*.

Short term and time limited

One distinctive feature of CBT is that it is comparatively time limited, being relatively short term, with most therapists typically offering between six and twenty sessions of CBT. This is in contrast to some psychoanalytic approaches which can be open-ended. The short-term nature of CBT has meant that it has been criticized for being a 'sticking plaster' or not addressing deeper issues. However, it makes CBT an attractive option to both patients and organizations that fund therapy services. A standard CBT intervention, for an individual rather than a group (group sessions tend to be longer), is usually between twelve and twenty sessions of fifty to sixty minutes, delivered on a weekly basis. Limited resources can mean that more minimal doses are offered with fewer sessions (e.g. six to ten) or shorter sessions. Shorter durations of therapy can be equally effective, especially for those with milder problems.

Critics of CBT argue that CBT's time-limited nature means that it may not be suitable for many patients such as those with more severe or complex problems, or those who struggle to articulate or concentrate. Indeed, research suggests that those with severe problems, and with co-morbid difficulties such as personality disorder, may need more than twenty sessions to gain the full benefit. And the length and frequency of CBT sessions may need to be adapted according to the individual's presentation or clinical need. For example, carrying out a particular therapeutic intervention, such as exposure to a specific setting, may necessitate a longer session. Or aspects of a patient's presentation, such as impaired concentration due to severe depression, may mean shorter more frequent sessions are more effective. The scheduling of sessions may also be modified in response to the patient's presentation, with sessions often being more frequent at the beginning of a course of therapy, especially for those with more severe problems, and tailing off to be fortnightly or monthly as the patient approaches recovery and is managing to use the CBT skills that they have learned to apply relatively independently.

Structured and collaborative

CBT is a structured approach, both within sessions as well as across the duration of a course of CBT. Structure is established from the beginning of each session by the patient and therapist collaborating to set an agenda for the session. Typically a session agenda will be a combination of one or two items specific to that session (a particular task that is identified as being a useful focus for the session) along with standard items that are covered in every session—checking the patient's current mood, reviewing of homework, feedback on the previous session, homework assignment, and feedback on the current session. The structured nature of CBT applies across the course of CBT too. In the earlier stages the focus is on information gathering, goal setting, developing a therapeutic alliance, and socialization to the CBT model. The middle phase involves developing a CBT formulation of the problem and using this to address current symptoms. Later stages in therapy may look at underlying beliefs and planning for relapse prevention. However, there is overlap between these phases (see Figure 18), and Figure 19 shows the iterative nature of the relationship between assessment and treatment in CBT.

Another fundamental principle of CBT's style is collaboration— any session or course of CBT should be a collaborative undertaking between the patient and therapist. A Chinese proverb says, 'Tell me and I forget. Teach me and I remember. Involve me and I learn.' Thus the therapist encourages the patient's active involvement at every level. The therapist and patient bring together their respective sources of expertise to try to understand and change the problem(s) that the patient wants help with. The patient and therapist collaborate at all stages of therapy—in the assessment and formulation to identify and understand the problem(s); in specifying the goals of therapy; in setting agendas

Session number									
1	2	3	4	5–12	13	14	15	16	Further follow ups
A/F	A/F	A/F							
S/G	S/G	S/G	S/G						
All.	All.	All.	All.						
		CT	CT	CT	CT	CT	CT		
				UB	UB	UB	UB	UB	
						RP	RP	RP	RP

A/F – Assessment and formulation
S/G – Socialization to the CBT model & goal setting
All. – building a therapeutic alliance
CT – active change techniques (see ch4)
UB – work on underlying beliefs such as dysfunctional assumptions and core beliefs
RP – relapse prevention

18. Typical activities across a course of CBT sessions.

for the sessions; in devising therapy tasks and between-session tasks ('homework'); in summarizing a shared understanding of what has been discussed; and in ending the therapy.

The collaborative nature of CBT may contrast with a more medical model, in which the doctor instructs the patient on what to do and the patient complies, to a greater or lesser degree, with the instructions. This means that patients may not be expecting to make such active contributions and may need to be encouraged to do so by the therapist. Often the therapist will offer more guidance in early sessions, but the patient is expected to take more responsibility for the sessions as they develop their CBT skills over the course of therapy. Socratic methods and guided discovery are used to enhance collaboration. Rather than telling the patient how it is, CBT therapists use Socratic questions to explore alternative perspectives on the issue. For example, asking if there are other ways of seeing the situation, or if a particular viewpoint applies in all situations, or how they would view the situation if it were a loved one, or how they might have viewed this situation before they became depressed. To enhance collaboration CBT therapists also use frequent summaries, and regularly seek feedback from the patient to check that they have a shared understanding of the relevant issues. At the end of the session the therapist typically asks the patient to summarize their understanding of what has

The style and structure of CBT

45

been covered, and how they will use it, and if anything was particularly helpful or unhelpful about the session. It is particularly important to be aware of any reservations that the patient has, as not only are these likely to impair progress, they may also damage the therapeutic relationship. If the patient does not feel that the therapist has fully understood their perspective, then they are less likely to see the therapist's suggestions as relevant or likely to be helpful. Using two-way feedback checks that the therapist and patient have understood each other and are both on the same page, aligned in working against the problem.

Empirical

CBT is an empirical approach, both within and across sessions. At the most fundamental level it is founded on the idea of evidence-based practice—that is, using the current best research evidence to make decisions in the care of individual patients. National guidelines exist to advise healthcare professionals about which treatments have the best evidence for which conditions. In the UK, the National Institute for Health and Care Excellence makes recommendations about which interventions have the best evidence for a particular condition, and they recommend CBT for a range of problems including anxiety and depression, as well eating disorders, post-traumatic stress disorder, psychosis, and bipolar disorder. Similarly, Cochrane is an independent charity that produces reviews of worldwide current best evidence to guide practitioners in deciding what interventions to offer.

While CBT is empirical in that it is evaluated by research, it is worth noting that the research is not perfect. While randomized controlled trials (RCTs) are considered the 'gold standard' in outcome research, they also have their problems, and can be flawed, inconclusive, or difficult to interpret. A typical RCT randomly allocates patients to two or more groups (e.g. treatment A vs treatment B vs control group/placebo) and compares their outcomes. The *experimental group* receives the treatment being

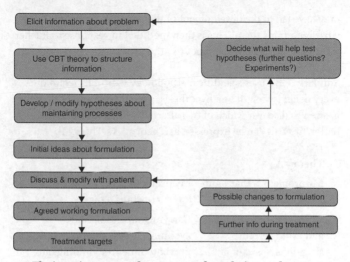

19. The iterative nature of assessment, formulation, and treatment in CBT.

evaluated, while the other group or groups provide some form of comparison (*control group*). To avoid bias participants are randomly allocated to groups, and ideally those assessing the outcomes are 'blind' to which group the patient is in. However, it is difficult to be 'blind' to the treatment condition with psychological treatments, and similarly there is no obvious placebo condition which has the same credibility as a psychological treatment. RCTs are time consuming and expensive to run, and their quality is variable, with factors such as investigator allegiance, therapist competence, inadequate longer term follow up, variable drop-out rates, and attrition all being sources of bias.

CBT is also aims to be empirical in using the scientific method within therapy, both within individual sessions as well as across the course of treatment. At the initial stages, the process of CBT assessment, formulation, and treatment is an iterative one in that the formulation is proposed as a working hypothesis about what may have led to the development of the patient's problem(s) and what maintains them. This is then modified in response to further information gained throughout treatment.

Similarly, CBT uses scientific methodology within its techniques—every belief is viewed as a hypothesis, and the purpose of therapy is often to discover which of two alternative hypotheses are a better 'fit'. This can be expressed as Theory A vs Theory B:

Theory A	Theory B
My problem is that I am in constant danger	My problem is my belief that I am in constant danger
Unless I carry out rituals and avoid certain situations, disaster is certain to occur	Carrying out rituals and avoiding certain situations has prevented me from finding out that disaster would not occur even if I did not do these things. Plus they are burdensome to do and stop me from living my life in the way that I want to.

Once a personalized version of Theory A and Theory B have been specified then therapy can be focused on discovering or testing out which of these competing hypotheses is a more accurate, and helpful, account of the patient's experience. Every belief or idea, expressed by either the patient or therapist, is viewed as a hypothesis that is amenable to testing. For example, if the patient expresses self-critical beliefs, the therapist will encourage the patient to actively seek out evidence to the contrary of these beliefs and incorporate that into a broader view.

CBT is also empirical in its reliance on measurement. Both within and across sessions CBT aims to measure relevant targets in order to assess change. For example, if the therapist and patient are working on re-evaluating a specific belief, hypothesized to be pertinent to the patient's current difficulties, then they will assess change by rating the patient's degree of conviction in that belief. This is a measure used to assess change within a given session, pre and post carrying out a specific targeted intervention. At the most basic level such measures may be 0–10 ratings of feelings, belief conviction, physiological states, or behavioural urges. At a more sophisticated level CBT therapists may use standardized, psychometrically validated measures. Standardized questionnaires exist to measure the severity of symptoms for all common mental health disorders and CBT therapists typically ask patients to complete these on a regular basis. They are used either to establish severity of symptoms (like taking a temperature) or more often to assess whether symptoms are improving as treatment progresses.

Questionnaires and other paper and pencil measures are good at measuring the more cognitive aspects such as degree of belief or severity of symptoms, but given CBT's equal emphasis on behaviour it is also useful to have behavioural measures. These may be ratings of how frequently a behaviour occurs (e.g. binge eating or purging), or the amount of time spent engaging in a behaviour (e.g. checking or hair pulling), or the number of times a behaviour is avoided. For accuracy of measurement, the closer to when the behaviour or thought occurred, the more accurate the recording is likely to be. Thus it is important that the patient has a discreet, portable way of recording relevant aspects between sessions, which can be anything from frequency counts in a diary, to paper or electronic notes.

Problem/goal focused

Unlike some forms of psychotherapy, CBT does not specifically focus on the individual's personality or experiences. Instead it is *problem focused*; it focuses on the specific problem(s) that the patient currently wants help with (assuming it is ethical to do so). This has raised concerns that CBT may be too simplistic or mechanistic, or fail to address the concerns of the 'whole' person. It is true that CBT usually does not attempt to 'fix' the person. Instead, it aims to help the individual to make changes in specific areas of their functioning. As part of the assessment the patient and therapist work together to gain a shared understanding of what the patient wants help with, they define the problem(s). The more detailed and specific this understanding is, the more useful it is in guiding therapy. So rather than just saying that the problem is depression, the therapist and patient construct a *problem list* of what specific aspects of depression are bothering them. The list is often a combination of symptoms of the problem, and consequences of those symptoms. See the box for an example.

Once the problem list has been identified the therapist and patient work together to specify the goals for therapy. These define the remit of therapy and specify exactly what the patient wants to

Problem list for depression

- Feeling sad. An average rating of 80 per cent sad in mornings and 60 per cent later in the day.
- Staying in bed too much (twelve to sixteen hours a day).
- Being signed off work and financial difficulties.
- Not seeing friends. Not going to book club or bowling.
- Difficulty concentrating. Not reading.
- Not enjoying anything (TV, reading, seeing friends, doing puzzles).
- Eating poor quality convenience food.
- Getting behind on household tasks (laundry, cleaning, paying bills).
- Not exercising and minimal dog walks.

achieve by the end of treatment—for example, to be less depressed. However, therapy goals, like most goals, are most useful when they are SMART (Specific, Measurable, Achievable, Relevant, and Time-related).

So a SMART goal relating to being less depressed might be to have an average mood rating of at least 5 out of 10, at least five days per week, by the end of therapy. See the box for an example. The therapist can help the patient to operationalize goals with Socratic questions such as 'how would you know when you were

SMART goals for depression

- Feel less than 50 per cent sad, on average, five days a week.

- Reduce time sleeping—set alarm (and get up) thirty minutes earlier every third day until getting up by 8 a.m. (for approximately six weeks).

- Contact friends via text or email and let them know that I am having a hard time but would welcome visitors.

- Arrange to meet J for a dog walk.

- Build concentration by reading paper, or news on Internet, for ten minutes at a time, at least once a day.

- Eat one nutritious meal every day. Preferably cooked from scratch. Aim for three portions of fruit/vegetables per day.

- Do online food shop on Sundays.

- Spend twenty minutes every morning and afternoon engaging in the most urgent household tasks (laundry, cleaning).

- Ask partner to take over paying bills for the moment.

- Start exercising by thirty-minute walk three times a week.

- Speak to employer about phased return to work once depressive symptoms have reduced by 50 per cent.

less depressed? What would you be able to do differently? How would you think or feel differently?' For example, they might know they were less depressed when they were getting out of bed by a certain time each day, or were socializing more frequently. It is also important that goals are realistic—if someone has been severely depressed for years it is unlikely that they will be completely better in three weeks' time, or that they will never suffer a moment of low mood again. If goals are not realistic it could lead to a setback or trigger feelings of hopelessness if they are not achieved. Thus, for the more severely impaired, it may be useful to break bigger goals down into a series of smaller more achievable steps.

SMART goals make explicit what the patient and therapist are working towards and allow both to evaluate whether progress is being made. Difficulties can arise when the therapist and patient do not agree on the target of the goals (e.g. weight loss for a patient who is already underweight) or when the patient's goals are beyond the remit of what CBT can realistically achieve (e.g. to find a partner). It may then be necessary to negotiate a compromise that is acceptable to both patient and therapist, and within the remit of CBT. For example, to reduce social anxiety such that the patient is comfortable initiating contact on Internet dating sites, or for the patient to be less distressed by maintaining a body weight in the healthy range.

Accessible and skills based

The philosophy underlying CBT, and the collaborative nature of the relationship between patient and therapist, mean that the therapist does not 'cure' the patient. Rather the therapist's role is to facilitate the patient in understanding CBT theory, and the formulation of their difficulties, and learn to use CBT skills, in order to enable them to address their own problems. Because of the focus on learning skills in CBT, between-session practice or homework assignments is an essential component—it is the training ground for the patient to practice their newly developed skills, with the weekly sessions with the therapist acting as consultations for the patient to review and refine their skills. Thus, an essential component of CBT is that the patient practises using what has been learnt in the sessions in their day-to-day life. So if in the session they are working on identifying relevant thoughts, the patient may be asked to keep a note of what was going through their mind every time they notice themselves experiencing a mood shift, that is, a discernible change in emotion such as anxiety or depression. Whether or not they are able to complete the task, it is likely to provide useful information. If they cannot complete the task then the therapist will explore and problem solve what made it difficult for them, which may lead to the task being changed or to elaboration of the formulation, as they will have identified an obstacle to change. Alternatively, if they are able to complete the task and identify their relevant thoughts then they can move on to looking at re-evaluating those thoughts.

Homework tasks often involve trying out doing something differently. For example, working up an exposure hierarchy. So someone with agoraphobia may be gradually increasing the amount of time that they spend outside of their home, and the distance they go. Indeed many behavioural assignments are not possible to carry out within the therapy session, as they require a specific setting or set of circumstances, such as a crowded shopping centre or a tall building, or the presence of particular people. Such assignments can be carried out as homework tasks and provide the ideal opportunity to put what the patient has learned into practice. The outcome of homework is reviewed in the next session. If for any reason the therapist neglects to review the homework tasks then they are sending a potentially unhelpful message to the patient—that the homework tasks are not important / it doesn't matter if they aren't completed. This is dangerous, as research evidence suggests that those who complete homework tasks are more likely to benefit from CBT than those who do not. So homework tasks should be collaboratively devised and well-planned; appropriate, relevant, and tailored to the patient's context; carried out in the context of a clear therapeutic rationale and sound relationship; and thoroughly reviewed, to help the patient identify what they have learned from the task and how they will use that going forward.

Homework tasks are best devised collaboratively during the session, with the patient making a note of the task and having the opportunity to ask questions or consider alternatives. Before the session ends the therapist will ask the patient to summarize the homework tasks, and the rationale for them.

Examples of homework tasks in CBT

- Complete questionnaires to measure symptoms.
- Listen to an audio recording of the session and summarize what was covered and what was learnt from it, in writing.
- Use worksheet to record thoughts and feelings in upsetting situations.
- Practise relaxation skills for thirty minutes a day.
- Use worksheet to evaluate evidence for and against a particular belief.
- Use worksheet to log activities and rate for pleasure and achievement.
- Use worksheet to plan activities that will be pleasurable and/ or give a sense of achievement.
- Carry out an exposure task, for example, if they are afraid of bees, look at pictures of bees in a book.
- Practising being assertive by telling a friend that you are not able to help them on this occasion.
- Prioritizing your own needs by spending time looking after yourself.

The therapist should also enquire as to any potential blocks to the patient being able to carry out the task, or any reservations they have about doing so. This gives the opportunity to problem solve potential obstacles or modify the task in the light of significant reservations.

As a skills-based approach, CBT also involves informing or educating the patient about psychological phenomena. Often this has the intention of normalizing the patient's experience. For example, most people experience intrusive thoughts or a degree of social anxiety in situations such as public speaking. Knowing that such experiences are commonplace may help to alleviate both anxiety and shame. Many anxiety disorders involve the maintenance cycle of being anxious about experiencing anxiety symptoms so education about the nature of anxiety can be helpful. Similarly, it can be helpful to gain insight into how common depression is and what the main symptoms are, so that the patient may be able to understand that hopelessness, difficulty concentrating, and fatigue may all be symptoms of depression rather than being due to personal weakness. Alternatively, the education may be targeted to a patient's specific concerns—for example, if a patient fears choking on their vomit it may be useful to gain information on the circumstances in which this is likely to occur (i.e. when the cough and gag reflexes are significantly suppressed). Now that we have looked at the style and structure of CBT, the way in which it is delivered, Chapter 5 will outline some of the main methods that CBT uses to achieve its aims.

Chapter 5
CBT methods

It has been said that CBT is the magpie of psychotherapy in that it 'borrows' (steals) the brightest and shiniest objects (techniques) from its fellow psychotherapies. Indeed, it is rumoured that Aaron T. Beck once claimed, 'if it works it's CBT'. So it is difficult to specify precisely what counts as a CBT method. Indeed, it could be argued that it is the underlying rationale, rather than the technique itself, that defines it as a CBT method—that is, when the therapy is carried out with the intention of impacting some aspect of cognition or behaviour in order to alleviate distress. This chapter outlines some of the main methods used to achieve change in CBT.

Cognitive techniques

Elizabeth Gilbert's (2006) observation that 'Your emotions are the slaves of your thoughts, and you are the slave of your emotions' reflects the fundamental idea behind CBT—that how you perceive a situation influences how you feel in that situation. When an emotional reaction seems out of proportion to the situation, and is distressing, CBT aims to understand the individual's idiosyncratic meaning attached to the situation in order to reduce their distress by helping them to change their interpretation of it (Figure 20).

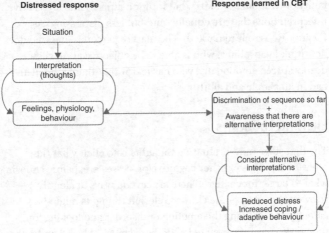

Distressed response   **Response learned in CBT**

20. **The role of interpretation.**

The primary purpose of cognitive techniques is to re-evaluate cognitive factors (thoughts, thinking styles, images) that are hypothesized (in the formulation) to be maintaining the problem(s). CBT does not aim to rid the individual of all irrational thoughts. Indeed, it would be unusual not to have any irrational thoughts. For example, most people have some superstitious beliefs (e.g. a lucky number) or irrational fears. The difference is that they are not unduly distressed by them. And research suggests depressed people may actually make more accurate predictions (*depressive realism*) than non-depressed people in certain circumstances. So rather than trying to eradicate irrational thinking, what CBT aims to do is to identify problematic beliefs that are hypothesized to be related to the difficulties that the individual wants help with; then examine the basis for these beliefs; and, if appropriate, help the person to find an alternative, less distressing perspective that is a better (or at least equally viable) account for the evidence. So, CBT does not aim to correct faulty or irrational thinking, but rather it aims to find alternative interpretations that are equally valid but less distressing. As Eleanor Roosevelt remarked, 'The mature person is one who does not think in absolutes, who is able to be objective even when deeply stirred emotionally, who has learnt that there is good and bad in all people and all things'.

Eliciting thoughts

The first stage in re-evaluating thoughts is to elicit what the relevant thoughts or other cognitive processes are, before choosing what to target for change. There are several ways to identify relevant thoughts. Some clues to relevant thoughts might be gained from knowing the emotion or disorder and looking for thoughts typically associated with those states. Tables 3 and 4 show typical thoughts associated with different emotions and disorders.

One of the most frequently used methods for identifying relevant thoughts is to ask the patient to recount a recent, vivid, experience of the problem affecting them. When they recount this episode in detail, the therapist probes for what was going through their mind at the time. This may be facilitated by asking the patient to try to

Table 3. Typical themes associated with different emotional states

Feeling	Typical themes in thoughts
Depression/sadness	Loss, hopelessness, self-criticism. The world is a bad place. The future is bleak.
Anxiety/fear	Perception of threat or danger—something bad will happen.
Anger	Perceived violation of the rules or acceptable standards by others. Unfairness. Injustice.
Guilt/shame	Violation of rules or acceptable standards by the self. Shame, particularly with the knowledge that others may be aware of the transgression.

Table 4. Typical themes associated with disorders

Disorder	Typical themes in thoughts
Panic disorder	Catastrophic misinterpretations of body sensations (e.g. 'I have palpitations, this is a sign I'm about to have a heart attack').
Health anxiety	Similar to panic disorder but less imminent / spread over a longer time span (e.g. 'these pins and needles could be an early sign of multiple sclerosis'; 'this mole could develop into skin cancer').
Obsessions and compulsions	Misinterpretations of intrusive thoughts, often as a sign of responsibility for preventing harm occurring (e.g. 'if I have these immoral thoughts it means I am a bad person and will go to hell'; 'if I can't be certain it's clean it could be contaminated / cause harm').
Social anxiety	Negative interpretations and evaluations of others' reactions (e.g. 'they will think I'm odd').
Phobias	Negative interpretations of the phobic stimuli and fear of fear (e.g. 'the spider will touch me and I won't be able to cope').
Post-traumatic stress disorder	The trauma is interpreted as a future threat (e.g. 'because it happened once it is likely to happen again'; 'the fact that I can't stop thinking about it means I will never go back to my normal self').
Relationship difficulties	Mismatched standards/expectations and negative interpretations of the other's intentions/behaviour (e.g. 'she leaves her stuff lying around because she does not care about me').

recreate the experience in their mind's eye and give a blow-by-blow account. Or the therapist may set up a situation in the therapy session that activates the problem. For instance, asking a socially anxious patient to give a short speech to a few colleagues; or a spider phobic to look at pictures of spiders. Another common method for identifying relevant thoughts is to ask the patient to keep a record, between sessions, of what goes through their mind when the problem is triggered, that is, when they notice a change in their mood (mood shift). The record is often kept by completing the first three columns of a *thought record*, which details the situation, feeling, and thought, and is subsequently used for re-evaluating thoughts (see Figure 22).

A further technique for identifying relevant thoughts is what is known as the *downward arrow technique* (see Figure 21). Thoughts can be like onions in that they may have many layers to be peeled away until you reach the most central part. The outer layer of thoughts may only describe avoidance-related thoughts (e.g. 'I need to get out of here') and the downward arrow technique aims to reveal the implications of the thought—what

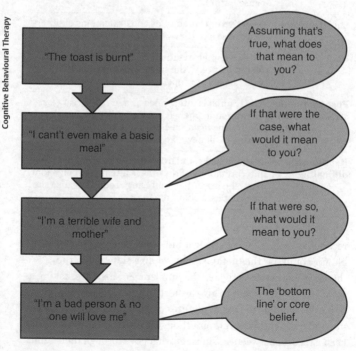

21. Example of downward arrow technique.

the person fears might happen if they are unable to get out of that particular situation.

Figure 21 shows how a reaction to something as trivial as burning toast can be underpinned by much more generalized and personally relevant beliefs, hence accounting for a more extreme emotional reaction than might be expected from simply burning toast.

Which thought?

Once relevant thoughts have been identified, the next stage is to choose which thought(s) to target for intervention. This can be one of the trickiest decisions for CBT therapists and is often not clear-cut. Several factors—whether it is really a thought or belief, whether it is representative and relevant, the level of distress caused, whether it is amenable to change, and whether it is best tackled at that particular stage of treatment are all factors guiding the choice of which thought to challenge; and these are laid out more fully in Table 5. Fortunately this is not a decision that you only get one chance at—a course of CBT will involve challenging many different thoughts, and ultimately aims to teach the method so the patient can challenge their own distressing thoughts.

Many thoughts are initially expressed as questions (e.g. 'What if I get it wrong?') and these become much more amenable to re-evaluation if they are phrased as a statement rather that a question (i.e. 'I will get it wrong'). The more fully the negative prediction can be specific the better—one person's 'wrong' will be different from another's. So the patient is encouraged to specify exactly what they think may go wrong, and how this will show itself, and what they fear the consequences might be. The degree to which they believe these things is relevant too—if I think there is only a 2 per cent chance that I will make a fool of myself then I would be much less anxious than if I believed it was 95 per cent

Table 5. Factors influencing the choice of which thought to challenge

Is it a thought?	It is preferable to challenge thoughts, as opposed to a statement of fact (e.g. 'I lost my job today') or feelings (e.g. 'I'm scared'). Feelings generally shouldn't be challenged—if the person feels that they are miserable or terrified, then, of course, they are! Rather than challenging their emotional experience, it can be more productive to focus on their interpretation of the implications of this (e.g. 'I will never feel better' or 'It's intolerable to feel this way'), or their predictions about the consequences of feelings (e.g. 'if I can't control my anxiety I will go crazy').
Is it representative and relevant?	We have many irrational thoughts but not all are relevant to the presenting problem, or typical of that person. So useful questions to consider are what thoughts go through a patient's mind when they are actually experiencing a particular problem (as opposed to when they are sitting in the therapist's office discussing the problem). Does the thought relate to the presenting problem? In anxiety, the focus would be on themes of danger/threat, whereas in depression, the relevant thoughts may be about loss, hopelessness, and self-criticism. Does the thought represent a repeating theme or is it a one off that has no broader relevance outside of a specific situation?
Is it sufficiently distressing?	Does this thought cause significant distress? Does the patient believe this thought strongly? If it is not significantly distressing, or strongly believed, then it may not be contributing enough to the presenting problem to be a priority for the session time.
Is it amenable to change?	Is the thought significantly distorted? Is it amenable to re-evaluation? If not problem solving may be a better option. Some thoughts are not very amenable to challenge (e.g. 'I will rot in hell for my sins').

Is it clinically appropriate to challenge this thought?	Is it appropriate to focus on this thought at this stage in treatment? Automatic thoughts are tackled earlier in treatment, while the more difficult to change assumptions and core beliefs are tackled later, once the patient has had the opportunity to develop their CBT skills somewhat. Is the patient stable and well-supported enough to begin to focus on this issue now? Is there sufficient time to deal with what may arise? It is not ideal to begin a discussion about a very upsetting issue in the last ten minutes of a session.

likely. So it is important to specify the thought in as much detail as possible, and to assess the degree to which the patient believes it when they are in the relevant situation. This latter assessment is particularly important as, when we are not in the relevant situation or experiencing the relevant emotion, we may have a much lower degree of conviction in the relevant beliefs. For example, I am aware that the consequences of performing poorly when public speaking are minimal in my current professional role, but this doesn't stop me from fearing public humiliation when I approach the podium! Anxiety tends to peak immediately prior to entering the situation and this is the ideal time to identify relevant thoughts and assess the degree of conviction in them.

Thinking styles

As well as looking at interpretations that are typical in each disorder, *thinking styles* may also have a role in maintaining emotional disorders. For example, a dichotomous thinking style, that is, seeing things as black or white, is likely to lead to more extreme emotional reactions because if it's not 'good' then it's 'awful'. Similarly, always thinking the worst, sometimes called catastrophizing, is likely to lead to more extreme negative reactions. Table 6 shows some of the thinking styles that may play a role in maintaining emotional difficulties.

Table 6. Characteristic thinking styles that may have a role in maintaining emotional distress

Thinking style	Description	Example
Dichotomous	Black and white thinking.	If it is not a total success, then it is a failure. If it's not perfect, then it's terrible.
Personalizing	Assuming everything is to do with you; taking too much responsibility for negative events.	The fact our team's performance wasn't great is all my fault. If the conversation doesn't flow smoothly that is entirely my responsibility.
Overgeneralization	Drawing sweeping conclusions from a single incident.	Not passing my driving test on the first attempt means that I will never succeed at anything in life. If X doesn't like me, no one ever will.
Selective thinking	Focusing on only part, usually the negative part, of the available information.	Ignoring the fact that you did well in all your exams and only focusing on the one that didn't go as well.
Catastrophizing	Overestimating and exaggerating the likely negative consequences.	Thinking that if you forgot to turn one plug socket off then the house will burn down and everyone will die.
Arbitrary inference	Drawing negative conclusions based on insufficient evidence.	Because they looked away it must mean that they noticed how anxious I was and were embarrassed.

Emotional reasoning	Making assumptions on the basis of one's feelings—assuming that feelings equate to reality.	I feel bad so I must be bad. I feel scared so it must be dangerous. I feel guilty so I must have done something wrong. I don't feel confident therefore I'm not capable.
Compare and despair	Comparing yourself to innumerable others, on innumerable variables, and only noticing the ways in which you fall short.	Everyone else is happier than me, has a better life, car, house, job, relationship, etc. Social media is an excellent way of feeding this one.
Fortune telling	Thinking that we can predict accurately what will happen in the future.	Because I made that mistake, I'm going to be fired. I'll never find another job.

Changing thinking

Once the therapist and patient have collaboratively agreed on a thought to target for re-evaluation there are several different techniques that can be used to achieve this aim. One of the cornerstone techniques is the process of Socratic questioning or the Socratic method, which can also be called *guided discovery*. Socratic questioning was named after the philosopher Socrates who, rather than answering his students' queries directly, used a series of exploratory, considered questions to guide them to discover the answer for themselves. The Socratic method is a way of facilitating the patient (or student, as was the case for Socrates) to consider a range of alternative interpretations that they are not currently aware of and use these to re-evaluate a previously held belief. This can be done using structured worksheets such as the *thought record*, outlined below, to evaluate the evidence for and against their current belief before formulating an alternative perspective. Or it can be done in a less structured way by using a Socratic style of questioning. Socratic questioning involves the following stages:

1. Asking informational questions to clarify understanding of the situation. *What situations do you feel worst in? How does that affect you?*

2. Empathic listening. Careful non-judgemental attention to what the patient is saying and any observed emotional reactions that go along with it. *It sounds like situations in which you feel negatively evaluated are really difficult for you. How do they make you feel?*

3. Summarizing and checking your understanding. *It seems that feeling judged makes you question yourself—is that right? It looks like those situations make you feel badly about yourself. In any particular respect?*

4. Synthesizing or analytical questions designed to broaden the patient's perspective to include information that they may not currently be aware of. *Are there any situations in which you don't feel judged? Or occasions where you have felt less judged? Or coped better with feeling judged? What was different about these times? What can we learn from that?*

Socratic questioning can be used to 'loosen' the patient's thinking, in combination with thought records, and prior to using more structured methods such behavioural experiments.

Thought records

The purpose of completing thought records should be further reaching than solely the impact of having re-evaluated one specific thought. First, re-evaluating thoughts by any method should help to create distance from the patient's current (distressing) perspective in that it is consistent with *meta awareness* of thoughts—the awareness that thoughts are just thoughts, not absolute facts. Second, using a thought record to re-evaluate any specific thought helps the patient to learn the method; and once the patient learns to use the method independently, it gives them a skill for re-evaluating distressing thoughts, and discovering alternative perspectives, that they can use across a variety of situations.

Usually a thought record (see Figures 22 and 23) is introduced in two or more stages, with the therapist supporting the patient to master each stage before progressing to the next stage. Initially the first three columns are completed—to note the date, time, and situation that triggered the emotional response, then to identify corresponding feeling(s) and the thoughts in that situation. Both feelings and thoughts are rated for intensity—the scale doesn't really matter as long as it is used consistently but often a 0–10 or 0–100 scale is used.

Once the patient is confident identifying the situation, their feelings, and their thoughts, the next stage is to choose a thought for re-evaluation. As noted above, this choice will be guided by several factors, including which thought is most distressing to the patient, sometimes called the *hot thought*. The thought record then asks the patient to list the evidence in support of the thought. It is unlikely that the patient would believe this thought in the absence of any evidence; and it is vital to know what you are trying to challenge before you try to challenge it ('know thine enemy', as the saying goes), so it is important that all the evidence for the thought is elicited before going on to examine the evidence against the thought.

Typically it is easier for people to generate evidence that is consistent with their existing thoughts and beliefs than it is to find evidence that is contrary to them, so in the initial stages the patient may need prompting by the therapist to identify evidence contrary to their belief. Table 7 gives some examples of shifting perspectives that may be useful in drawing the patient's awareness to evidence that may not be consistent with their existing belief.

Cognitive Behavioural Therapy

Date / time / situation	Feeling(s) 0–100	Automatic Thoughts (Images)	Evidence that supports that thought	Evidence that does not support that thought	Alternative/ balanced thought	Re-rate feelings 0–100
		1. What was going through your mind before you started to feel this way? Any other thoughts or images? 2. How much did you believe this? 0-100 3. Which thought bothers you most?			Write an alternative balanced thought. Rate how much you believe the alternative balanced thought (0–100%)	

22. Standard seven-column thought record.

Table 7. Shifting perspectives to find alternatives

Shift in person	What would I say to a friend or someone I care about who was in the same situation?
	What would I like someone who cared about me to say to me to support and encourage me?
Shift emotional frame of reference	How would I see this if I was not depressed/anxious?
	If I'm being warm and compassionate towards myself, what might I think instead?
	When I am not in the situation do I see it differently?
Shift in time frame of reference	A few months ago, before I was depressed, how would I have thought about this?
	Imagine that, in a year's time, I'm looking back at this situation—what advice would I be giving myself?
	Have there been times when I didn't feel this way? Or times this belief did not apply?
	What will I think looking back on this in ten years' time?

Once evidence has been generated for and against the belief that is being re-evaluated the next stage is to formulate an alternative perspective, also called a *balanced alternative* because it aims to take into account both the evidence for, and against, the original belief. Figure 23 shows an example of a completed thought record.

Once a thought record has been completed it is unlikely that the degree of conviction in the original belief will have reduced to 0 or that the degree of conviction in the alternative will be 100. A thought record may have to be repeated many times, across a variety of situations, for significant belief change to occur. And even then, it may remain hypothetical—there is likely to be remaining uncertainty, so the next stage is to consider how to further differentiate between the two beliefs. One way that this can be done is to devise ways to test out the new belief in action, or to directly compare which belief is a better account of the patient's experience.

Date / time / situation	Feeling(s) 0-100	Automatic Thoughts (Images) 1. What was going through your mind before you started to feel this way? Any other thoughts or images? 2. How much did you believe this? 0-100 3. Which thought bothers you most?	Evidence that supports that thought	Evidence that does not support that thought	Alternative/ balanced thoughts. Write an alternative balanced thought. Rate how much you believe in each alternative balanced thought (0-100%)	Re-rate feelings 0-100
Tuesday lunchtime. Supermarket shopping.	Hot, sweaty, shaky, rapid breathing and heart rate. **Anxiety 90** **Panic 60**	I'm going to have a panic attack and I won't be able to control it. 90 **I might pass out. 60** People will think I'm crazy. 90 I will be locked up. 70	I feel so ill – the physical symptoms are overwhelming and escalate really fast. My legs feel like jelly. I feel like I might faint. Some people do pass out or faint sometimes.	I have had hundreds of panic attacks but never passed out. In order to faint your blood pressure needs to drop and my rapid heart rate means my blood pressure is increasing not falling. Even if I did faint I might not be locked up—most people who faint are offered help, not locked up. Lots of people have panic attacks but don't pass out.	The most likely explanation is that these are just really uncomfortable symptoms of escalating anxiety / panic which won't do me any harm. 40 I am not about to pass out. 60	**Anxiety 25** **Panic 10**

23. Completed thought record for a patient with panic disorder.

Behavioural techniques

By three methods we may learn wisdom: first, by reflection, which is noblest; second, by imitation, which is easiest; and third by experience, which is the bitterest.

(Confucius 551–479 BC)

Before moving on to look at behavioural techniques in CBT it should be noted that there isn't a clear boundary between cognitive and behavioural techniques, and the best CBT interventions usually combine both elements. Chadwick, Birchwood, and Trower note that, 'Beliefs rarely change as a result of intellectual challenge, but only through engaging emotions and behaving in new ways that produce evidence that confirms new beliefs'. A good example of a behavioural intervention being used to consolidate cognitive change is a *behavioural experiment*. Kennerley, Kirk, and Westbrook describe behavioural experiments as planned experiential activities, based on experimentation or observation, which are undertaken by patients, in or between CBT sessions. Their design arises directly from the CBT formulation. Their primary purpose is: to obtain new information which may contribute to the development of the formulation; to test the validity of the patient's existing beliefs about themselves, others, and the world; or to construct and test new, more adaptive, beliefs.

Often behavioural experiments are used to extend the impact of verbal discussions such as Socratic questioning or thought records. Having explored a particular belief and generated alternative views through discussion, behavioural experiments provide a means of testing out or consolidating these conclusions. They can be a means of gathering evidence to help differentiate between the old and new beliefs. Alternatively, behavioural experiments can be done to generate new information or hypotheses. Mark Twain recognized the value of experiential learning in his unverified quote: 'if you hold a cat by the tail, you

CBT methods

71

learn things that cannot be learned in any other way'. Chapter 2 outlined some of the early behavioural interventions such as exposure and systematic desensitization. These interventions may look very similar to a behavioural experiment, indeed, the patient may be doing the exact same thing in each—such as going into a supermarket—but the rationale underlying the intervention is different, as outlined in the box containing examples of hypothesis driven experiments.

Preliminary evidence suggests that setting up exposure tasks as a behavioural experiment, that is, as a test of a particular belief, may be more effective than exposure alone. And data from memory studies suggest that experiential learning derived from real life experience with emotional content is processed at a deeper and more memorable level than purely factual information with Engelkamp concluding that 'Memory for actions that one has

How behavioural experiments differ from exposure

Exposure
- Based on behavioural theories of learning (classical conditioning)
- Mechanism of change is through prolonged exposure and repetition leading to habituation and eventually extinction of the anxiety response
- Primarily applicable to fear/ anxiety
- No attention paid to beliefs
- For example, going into the supermarket and staying there until anxiety decreases by 50 per cent.

Behavioural experiment
- Based on cognitive theory—aims to verify or falsify beliefs
- Mechanism of change is through changing beliefs so repetition not necessary, but may be needed across different situations or contexts
- Applicable across range of disorders
- For example, going into the supermarket and staying there long enough to find out whether you will faint.

observed...or that one has only heard about...is less good than memory for self-performed actions'.

Behavioural experiments may be a particularly powerful form of learning as they incorporate all the stages of experiential learning such as planning, observation, being actively involved, and reflection on the experience. Behavioural experiments can be hypothesis driven or discovery orientated. Discovery orientated experiments aim to generate data—to find out what might happen in a given situation. They are often observational and can involve data gathering. For example, what is the actual likelihood of being killed on any given plane journey? Or what is the average body mass index of a middle-aged female in the USA? This may involve research or surveys. Surveys can be a good way of discovering information about what others notice, or how they interpret things such as showing signs of anxiety. So if a patient feared that their hands would tremble and that other people might then think they were an alcoholic, it may be useful to construct a survey about how they themselves would interpret seeing someone else's hand shaking. This method can also be useful in body dysmorphic disorder (where the patient has an overly negative perception of some aspect of their physical experience). An example would be to have a series of photos of a range of people and ask survey participants to identify if any of them stood out as looking unusual and, if so, why. Often the photo of the patient is not selected and, if it is, it is often not for the reason the patient feared.

Hypothesis driven experiments are more like experiments in science where you have a specific hypothesis that you are seeking to confirm or refute. They are used when a patient has a clear prediction about what will or won't happen (e.g. 'I will faint') whereas discovery orientated experiments are useful when you want to find out what might happen (e.g. 'what will happen if I don't try to please people?').

Examples of hypothesis driven experiments

Testing old beliefs (hypothesis A)

'If I ask for help, I will be mocked'

Experiment: Ask partner if she can take me to garage to collect car and see how she responds.

Testing new beliefs (hypothesis B)

'Re-engaging with neglected activities will help my mood'

Experiment: Spend thirty minutes gardening twice a day and monitor mood.

Comparing two different beliefs (hypothesis A vs hypothesis B)

'Do people look at me because I'm weird, or just because they look at everyone?'

Experiment: Count how many people turn to look when I enter a cafe and how many people turn to look when others enter.

Experiments can be an excellent way of changing beliefs about the consequences of anxiety symptoms. Predictions such as 'I will faint / pass out / vomit' are very amenable to testing. Often the therapist would model the experiment first by feigning the symptom (e.g. by pretending to faint in a public place), with the patient observing the consequences. Then the patient would be asked to carry out the experiment, ideally with the therapist observing. Doing any experiment once is unlikely to lead to complete belief change—it may need to be repeated across situations, people, and time for the patient to be fully confident of the real likely consequences. For this reason it is useful for patients to learn to carry out behavioural experiments independently. Worksheets such as the one shown in Figure 24 can be a useful guide to structuring the planning, carrying out, and reflecting on behavioural experiments. Careful planning increases the likelihood of behavioural experiments generating useful data. First both the patient and the therapist must be clear about the purpose of the experiment—is it to test a specific belief? Or just to see what would happen—for example, if you do something you have previously avoided or behave in a different way? If relevant, a specific prediction needs to be made as well as specifying a way to know whether the prediction has been realized or not. Then the patient and therapist try to come up with a situation that will test that prediction. This may involve specifying not only location or situation but other relevant factors too such as other people present. The difficulty of the experiment needs to be matched to the patient's current level of functioning—not so difficult that it is avoided or endured with intense distress, but difficult enough to be a challenge and activate the problem.

Ideally early behavioural experiments will be carried out with the therapist present to provide support and structure, with the patient moving on to carrying out experiments independently as therapy progresses and they become more confident in their skills. It is worth remembering that any behavioural experiment is a successive approximation to the ideal behavioural experiment—there will always be room for doubt and this doubt can be used to guide the next behavioural experiment. Thus carrying out behavioural experiments should be viewed as a journey, and it may be the journey rather than the destination that is most important: learning the method may be the most important factor. The ideal scenario is that whenever the patient is faced with doubt, or has the inclination to avoid a situation, they will respond by turning the situation into a behavioural experiment to clarify their doubt or find out if they have justification to fear the situation.

Cognitive Behavioural Therapy

Day	Target to be tested	Experiment	Prediction(s)	Outcome	What I learned
What thought, assumption or belief are you testing? Is there an alternative perspective? Rate conviction in beliefs (0–100)	*Design an experiment to test the belief (e.g. testing an anxious prediction, facing a situation you would otherwise avoid, dropping precautions, behaving in a new way)*	*What do you predict will happen? How will you know if this does / doesn't happen?*	*What actually happened? What did you observe? How does the outcome fit with your predictions?*	*What does this mean for your original belief? Or the alternative perspective? How far do you now believe it (0–100%). Does it need to be modified? How?*
Saturday	If my hand shakes while paying in a shop they will think I am committing fraud. (60%)	Purposefully shake hand when paying in grocery store.	They will look at me strangely. Call security. Request extra checks on my debit card.	Nobody seemed to pay any attention to it. They didn't call security, or phone the bank.	Maybe my shaking isn't as obvious as I think it is. Or not everyone interprets it as a sign of wrong doing. (90%)
Tuesday	If I appear nervous in the meeting people won't respect my views (90%)	Go to the meeting and don't do anything to hide my anxiety.	They will not be interested in listening to my views. People will talk over me to tell me to be quiet.	I was quite nervous in the meeting – trembling hands and sweating. Nobody seemed to pay any attention to it and they seemed to listen when I spoke. Only one person talked over me but she talked over everyone!	Despite being anxious people still listened to what I had to say and seemed to value it. (95%)

24. **Record sheet for behavioural experiments.**

Intervening on activity directly

Just as thought records and Socratic questioning are not the only cognitive techniques employed in CBT, behavioural experiments are just one of a range of behavioural interventions. Another is *activity scheduling*. Activity scheduling is based on the premise that how we spend our time will have a significant influence on our mood (feelings), thoughts, and physiology. As noted in Chapter 3, a common maintaining cycle in depression is low mood leading to a reduction of activity, which in turn means reduced opportunities for pleasure or a sense of achievement, which then further lowers mood. Activity scheduling aims to provide a structured way to break this cycle. The first stage involves the patient keeping a detailed record of how they are currently spending their time, and making ratings for how much pleasure (0–10) and achievement (0–10) they get from each activity.

Once the patient has been able to record information about how they are spending their time, this record is reviewed with the therapist. Areas to consider include how the patient is spending their time—are they doing too much? Or too little? Are they taking care of their physical needs—how is their sleep? Are they eating regularly? Having any exercise? How wide is their range of activities? Does it include a mix of obligations (e.g. work, chores, childcare) and relaxation? Is it all duties and no fun? Is there significant contact with other people? A second consideration is how their pattern of activities compares to what they did before they became unwell. What activities have they stopped doing? Are they doing more of anything? Is it all responsibilities and no pleasure? How much time is devoted to activities that would be expected to be enjoyable? Or give a sense of achievement? The therapist would also look for any obvious patterns in the relationship between activities and enjoyment or achievement—are certain times of the day better or worse? Or are particular activities, settings, or people more or less difficult? Finally, the therapist would question any ratings that don't seem to make sense—for example, activities that would be expected to be enjoyable but are not experienced as such. They would seek to understand what might be undermining the enjoyment of such activities.

This chapter has covered the core methods used in standard CBT. Chapter 6 goes on to look at the areas in which these have been applied.

Chapter 6
Applications of CBT

Early versions of behaviour therapy focused on exposure techniques for anxiety and the earliest versions of cognitive therapy targeted negative thinking in depression. Since the development of integrated cognitive and behavioural interventions in the 1960s and 1970s, CBT has been applied to an increasing range of areas. This chapter will give an overview of the range of problems and patient groups that CBT has been used with. As mentioned in Chapter 1, a large part of CBT's success has been due to its ability to evolve, which happens by the process of evidence-based practice shown in Figure 25.

One of the areas to which evidence-based practice has led CBT is the development of diagnosis-specific CBT models. The observations that patients with a particular anxiety disorder tended to interpret situations in similar ways led to the development of specific CBT models for formulating the different anxiety disorders. So rather than formulating and treating all anxiety disorders in the same way, based on their shared features, protocols have been developed to target the core cognitive distortions specific to the particular anxiety disorder. Such processes are hypothesized to be central in the maintenance of that specific diagnosis. One of the earliest diagnosis-specific models was for the understanding and treatment of panic

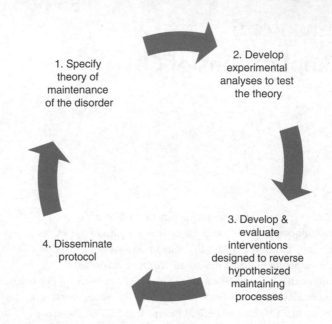

1. Specify theory of maintenance of the disorder

2. Develop experimental analyses to test the theory

3. Develop & evaluate interventions designed to reverse hypothesized maintaining processes

4. Disseminate protocol

25. The process of evidence-based practice.

disorder, and the development of CBT for panic disorder is a good example of the process of evidence-based practice.

The Oxford-based clinical psychologist, David M. Clark, observed that patients with panic disorder tended to *catastrophically misinterpret* their benign bodily sensation—that is, to interpret a bodily sensation as a sign of impending disaster. For example, an increase in heart rate might be interpreted as an impending heart attack as opposed to normal variation or benign interpretations such as exertion or too much caffeine. Similarly, a headache could be interpreted as a stroke. Or dizziness as a sign of imminent collapse. Often the sensations that were misinterpreted as signs of an imminent catastrophe were the physiological symptoms of anxiety itself (e.g. sweating, increased heart rate, shortness of breath, being hot, etc.) thus leading to a vicious cycle of escalating anxiety and physiological sensations. Based on such observations, in 1986, Clark proposed the cognitive model of panic disorder, one of the first diagnosis-specific CBT models.

Proposing a theory of the maintenance of the disorder is the first stage in the process of evidence-based practice shown in Figure 26. The next stage involves experimental tests of this theory—for example, experiments have found that patients with panic disorder have improved cardiac, but not gastric, awareness—suggesting that they do show increased attention to potentially threatening bodily sensations. Or that panic attacks can be brought on by administering a biological challenge, such as

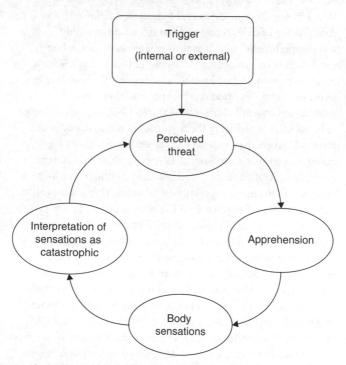

26. Clark's cognitive model of panic disorder.

carbon dioxide inhalation or lactate infusion, to induce unexpected bodily sensations. Such challenges only trigger panic attacks when the patient is not told that the symptoms that they are experiencing are a consequence of the biological challenge, that is, when they are not given an alternative, non-threatening, explanation for the symptoms.

Following on from the theory and experimental tests, the third stage in the cycle of evidence-based practice is to develop and evaluate an intervention that aims to reverse the hypothesized maintaining mechanisms. This is what CBT for panic disorder aims to do—to attenuate the patient's tendency to make catastrophic misinterpretations of benign bodily sensations. Which is usually done by careful formulation followed by a combination of challenging and testing out catastrophic misinterpretations, as well as testing alternative, more benign, explanations for symptoms. Protocols for panic typically then move on to reducing avoidance and exposure to feared bodily sensations, and the situations that provoke them. Several randomized controlled trials have shown CBT for panic disorder to be effective in reducing the frequency of panic attacks, with most patients being 'panic free' at the end of treatment and maintaining this over follow up. However, while results from carefully controlled randomized trials are an important source of evidence, they are not especially useful unless they can be rolled out into routine clinical care for the general population of people suffering from panic disorder. So the fourth stage of the process of evidence-based practice is for the protocol to be disseminated. It is one thing to show that a treatment is effective under ideal circumstances, but another to show that it is effective in routine clinical care. Dissemination of novel interventions, also called *implementation science*, is a particularly tricky area of research and is discussed further in Chapter 7. With regards to the CBT treatment of panic disorder, some inroads into dissemination have been made. For example, one study showed that clinicians got a larger proportion of patients 'panic free' after they had been given

training in CBT for panic than they had achieved prior to the
training, suggesting that CBT for panic disorder can be
successfully disseminated.

The process of rolling a treatment out into routine care can
provide opportunities for further development of the treatment.
The increased numbers and variation in people treated in routine
practice mean that the intervention may not get the same results
in routine practice as it did in the original research trials. Rather
than viewing this as a limitation or failure of the original
treatment, it can also be viewed as an opportunity for further
development of both the theory and the intervention. Before we
consider this further, it is worth considering the difference
between the efficacy and effectiveness of treatments.

Efficacy vs effectiveness of treatments

The *efficacy* of a treatment is the impact of the intervention
under the best possible conditions. In contrast the *effectiveness* is
the impact of the intervention under pragmatic or 'real life'
conditions, considering other factors such as the acceptability of
the intervention and compliance with it. So efficacy trials
determine the impact of the intervention under ideal
circumstances whereas effectiveness trials (pragmatic trials)
measure the impact of the intervention in real world settings.

There are several differences between efficacy trials and
effectiveness trials. In efficacy studies, efforts are made to
maximize *internal validity*, so typically there will be random
allocation to active or control conditions, and therapists will be
trained and certified to a specified level of competence. The
patients may have been actively selected for having only one
specific problem, and being a typical presentation of that

(continued)

Efficacy vs effectiveness of treatments Continued

problem. In contrast, effectiveness trials prioritize *external validity*, so seek to recruit cases that are representative of those seen in routine clinical practice, which may include those with co-morbid conditions and atypical presentations. Aspects of the intervention may also differ—in routine practice, therapists typically see a wide range of patient presentations ('all comers'), but in an efficacy trial the therapists may be experts at treating that one particular problem. Available resources may also differ—an efficacy trial aims to evaluate the impact of the treatment under ideal conditions—hence patients are offered the maximum dose of the treatment, by highly trained and supervised therapists. In contrast, effectiveness trials seek to evaluate how the treatment works in routine practice where there will be resource limitations, so therapists may be less expert in that particular intervention, the dose of treatment may be lower, and therapists' caseloads may be higher.

An example of the difference in efficacy vs effectiveness of an intervention is in those for weight loss. TV programmes focusing on extreme weight loss give participants a lot of expert and peer support to engage in exercise and adhere to a low calorie diet. The intervention—eating fewer calories and exercising more—is essentially following what a general practitioner (GP) would advise any overweight patient. However, the intensity at which it is offered, and the support for compliance that is provided, are markedly different. So dieting and exercising have demonstrated high efficacy in the treatment of obesity but have much lower effectiveness because most patients are not able to adhere to the intervention without the very high levels of support. This is similar to medications that are highly efficacious but where patients have difficulty in tolerating the side effects or following the highly restrictive regimens.

So what can happen is that a treatment appears to be less effective in real world settings than it was in the original efficacy trials—something has been lost in the translation. While initially disappointing, this can be used as an opportunity for further development. The observation that not all patients respond optimally to the treatment needs to be understood, which in turn may give rise to further elaboration of the underlying theory and resulting improvements in interventions. For example, observations of panic disorder patients who were not responding optimally led to extension of the cognitive theory of panic disorder. It was already known that avoiding anxiety provoking situations acted to maintain anxiety by preventing patients from finding out that their interpretations of bodily sensations were mistaken. However, careful study of the patients who were not responding to treatment led to the observation that while these patients seemed not to have been overtly avoiding a given situation, they may have been subtly avoiding particular aspects of it. In turn, this led to the incorporation of the concept of *safety seeking behaviours* into the cognitive model of panic as shown in Figure 27.

Safety seeking behaviours are behaviours by which a patient attempts to keep themself safe in a situation they perceive to be dangerous, but which actually act as subtle forms of avoidance, thereby preventing realization that in fact they are making catastrophic misinterpretations, and thus maintaining the problem. For example, if a patient fears they may have a heart attack they may take their own pulse to reassure themselves, and this reassurance reduces their anxiety, but it also prevents them from finding out that they would not have had a heart attack, regardless of whether pulse was raised or not. Or, if they fear what people may think of them for showing symptoms of anxiety in a particular situation, they may not avoid the situation entirely but instead take great care to control or conceal any anxiety symptoms when in that situation, for example avoiding having their hands on show (for fear that trembling will be visible). The increased

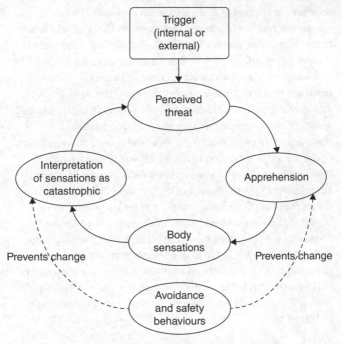

27. Revised cognitive model of panic disorder.

specificity of diagnosis specific models has led to changes in CBT protocols. For example, in panic disorder, the therapist will actively look for catastrophic misinterpretations of bodily sensations, as the underlying theory suggests these are critical in maintaining panic attacks, and be aware of the potential for subtle safety seeking behaviours to act as avoidance and thus undermine the effectiveness of exposure.

Experimental studies and treatment trials have generally been supportive of diagnosis-specific models. Consequently, such models have been proposed for many common mental health problems. For example, health anxiety is thought to be maintained by similar catastrophic misinterpretations of bodily sensations as in panic disorder, but over a longer timescale. So a tingling sensation in a patient's fingers could be misinterpreted as the early signs of multiple sclerosis rather than as an impending heart attack. Similarly, diagnosis-specific CBT models and protocols have been proposed, and received empirical support for the treatment of, other anxiety disorders including specific phobias, obsessive compulsive disorder, social phobia, and generalized anxiety disorder. The core misinterpretations thought to underlie those disorders of course vary. In phobias, the emphasis is on fear of the anxiety response itself, as well as danger-related beliefs about the source of the phobia, for instance that spiders are likely to bite. Social phobia also includes fear of anxiety symptoms but has more of an emphasis on how showing the symptoms of anxiety, or other supposed weaknesses, will be perceived by other people. Core cognitive themes in obsessive compulsive disorder vary depending on the nature of the primary concern (e.g. contamination vs checking) but centre on the theme of an overdeveloped sense of responsibility for the prevention of harm. The box gives examples of typical thoughts in the different anxiety disorders.

CBT and trauma

An area related to anxiety disorders to which CBT has been applied is in the treatment of *trauma*. What constitutes trauma is an area of debate, but a commonly accepted definition is an event involving actual or threatened death or serious injury, or a threat to the physical integrity of the self or others. *Post-traumatic stress disorder* (PTSD) is a common response to experiencing a traumatic event. It involves symptoms such as re-experiencing the event in flashbacks, intrusive thoughts or nightmares, significant avoidance of reminders of the trauma, symptoms of increased arousal (e.g. irritability, exaggerated startle, insomnia, difficulty concentrating) and negative changes in thought and mood (e.g. loss of interest, negative evaluations of the self/world/others, detachment, feelings of blame, or other negative emotions).

Typical thoughts in different anxiety disorders
Social phobia

'I'll sweat/shake/stutter'

'People will see I'm anxious . . . they will think less of me'

'I don't know what to say, I'll sound stupid'

'If people see the real me they will be critical / reject me'

Specific phobia

'Spiders are dangerous / disgusting'

'If the spider gets close to me I won't be able to cope'

'It will crawl into my mouth'

Obsessive compulsive disorder

'Germs are everywhere—I could be contaminated'

'If I don't check it could flood / catch fire'

'I can't be sure I locked it . . . it will be a disaster if I didn't'

Generalized anxiety disorder

'It could go wrong . . . it will be a disaster if it does'

'Uncertainty is terrifying'

'I must think ahead and try to anticipate anything that could go wrong'

'All this worrying is bad for me . . . I can't control it'

Panic disorder

'Unexplained body sensations are terrifying'

'I will panic and I won't be able to cope'

'I will pass out / have a heart attack / stroke / die'

Although previously classified as an anxiety disorder, the most recent classification (by the American Psychiatric Association) has moved PTSD to a separate category for 'Trauma and Stress-Related Disorders'. Trauma can occur in childhood or adult life and can be classified as Type I or Type II according to whether it is due to a single incident such as an accident or more prolonged circumstances, such as in combat or childhood sexual abuse.

Responses to trauma are hugely variable and PTSD is far from the only one. While many who experience trauma will show symptoms of PTSD, others may respond by becoming depressed or by developing more generalized anxiety or a specific phobia—for example, a phobia of driving following a road traffic accident. At a most fundamental level CBT conceptualizes anxiety as being driven by the perception of threat—the perception that something bad may happen in the future. What differentiates PTSD from other anxiety disorders is that the event provoking the anxiety, or trauma, is already in the past. Hence, what CBT models of PTSD aim to understand is how the trauma is being perceived as a current or future threat, and why this does not naturally attenuate with experience. While most people who have undergone a traumatic experience will initially respond by showing at least some symptoms of PTSD, the most common pattern is that of spontaneous recovery. That is, these symptoms will gradually abate with time. For example, one study showed that while 94 per cent of a sample of ninety-five rape victims experienced all of the symptoms necessary for the diagnosis of PTSD when assessed soon after the rape, by three months after the rape only 47 per cent of the women still met this criteria, meaning almost half had shown significant improvement in the absence of any treatment. Thus, there is a process of natural recovery following even the most extreme traumatic experiences, and what CBT models seek to understand is what interrupts that process for those people who continue to have symptoms. Clinical psychologists, Anke Ehlers and David M. Clark, proposed a CBT model of PTSD shown in Figure 28 which attempts to explain how PTSD symptoms are maintained.

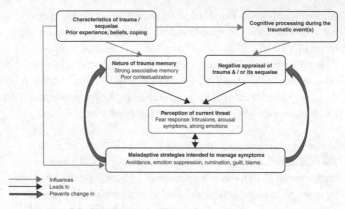

28. CBT model of PTSD.

Following on from CBT formulations of PTSD, specific versions of CBT interventions have been developed for treating PTSD symptoms. Cognitive components focus on identifying the way that the trauma is interpreted as a current threat, and on re-evaluating and testing out (where safe) those interpretations. Behavioural components focus on exposure to avoided aspects of the trauma, often by getting the patient to 'relive' the trauma by going over the memory repeatedly until anxiety habituates or corrective interpretation is incorporated. A common interpretation during a traumatic event is the perception of threat—for example, that you may die. Reliving the trauma can help the individual to incorporate into their traumatic memory the corrective information that, while they had feared that they would die at the time of the trauma, they in fact had not died. Another common source of threat in PTSD is in the interpretation of the sequelae of the trauma—the individual feels that they, or their life, or their perception of the world has fundamentally changed for the worse due to the trauma. For example, they may interpret their experience of PTSD symptoms as meaning that they are going crazy or are no longer the same person. Standard CBT techniques can be used to normalize the occurrence of PTSD symptoms following trauma and to challenge overly negative interpretations. However, it is important to recognize that there are many instances where a person's life may have been permanently negatively affected by the trauma. For instance, if there is a resultant ongoing disability, or pain, or loss of loved ones. In such circumstances, a broader formulation may be needed, which overlaps with the CBT approach developed for those in ongoing adverse life circumstances.

Coping with adversity

A common criticism of CBT is that its focus on correcting distorted appraisals means that it has little to offer those in adverse circumstances whose negative appraisals may be realistic. In recent years, CBT therapists such as psychiatrist Stirling Moorey have applied CBT models and techniques to those experiencing adverse life circumstance—for instance, to those with a diagnosis of terminal illness. Such approaches propose that serious life events and illness challenge our underlying beliefs about ourselves, the world, and the future. Adjustment to loss, injury, or illness involves a process of appraisal and reappraisal, and these appraisals will in turn influence coping strategies that can facilitate or hinder this process. CBT interventions aim to examine adaptive and maladaptive coping, and to help the person through the process of adjusting to their changed circumstances and make the best of their circumstances, however difficult they may be. Consideration is given to realistic negative thoughts and problem solving may be more appropriate than challenging such thoughts. The goal is to maximize opportunities and minimize suffering despite the circumstances. Often there is considerable overlap between adverse life circumstances and the experience of trauma (e.g. for asylum seekers) and a tailored formulation may be needed to incorporate both the traumatic experiences that have given rise to PTSD symptoms and the adverse circumstances that have given rise to current challenges. For example, Akosua sought asylum in the UK with her young son after experiencing and witnessing extreme violence in her country of origin. While she was relieved to be out of immediate danger, she continued to experience post-traumatic symptoms such as nightmares and flashbacks. She was terrified that she would bump into one of her abusers on the streets of London, or that her application to remain in the UK would be refused and she would be returned to her country or origin. Given her uncertain asylum status, it is easy to see how the perceived threat remained current. As Akosua had previously experienced violence and sexual trauma from authority figures (police, soldiers) she found it very difficult to trust people in positions of authority. In addition, English was not her first language, which meant she was very isolated in the UK, and struggled to gain employment. For Akosua, the therapist needed to take extra time to establish a trusting relationship (via an interpreter) and work on safety and stabilization before they could move on to attempting to treat the post-traumatic symptoms. The treatment of Akosua's trauma was further complicated by the real risk that she could be sent back to her country of origin if her asylum was not approved. In addition, daily life for Akosua was difficult—poor quality temporary accommodation, social isolation, and very limited finances presented daily challenges. The therapist worked with Akosua to problem solve some of these difficult life circumstances and make changes such as taking English language classes and making connections with other parents. This helped Akosua to become stable enough to be able to work on her post-traumatic symptoms directly.

Health-related behaviours

Following on from using CBT to help those in adverse life circumstances is its application to health-related behaviours. Currently, many of the biggest public health challenges, such as obesity and substance misuse, are influenced by our health-related behaviours, and as such should be amenable to behaviour change strategies. Similarly challenging is optimizing the management of long-term conditions, either by influencing health-related behaviours or via interventions that aim to facilitate treatment adherence, which may include enhancing medication adherence or lifestyle restrictions. In some ways the intervention is obvious— stop smoking, drink less alcohol, exercise more, eat less, and take medications as prescribed. However, data on longer term abstinence and weight loss, or on medication adherence, suggest that even modest weight loss is difficult to sustain and up to 50 per cent of prescribed medication is not taken. Hence, there remains considerable room for improvement.

While the obvious interventions such as stopping smoking or calorie restrictive diets have high efficacy, the effectiveness of these interventions, particularly in the longer term, is less established. In response to this challenge, CBT has focused on how to help make health-related behaviour change programmes more effective. Such behaviour change strategies require self-control, self-discipline, and sustained motivation, all of which should be amenable to change through CBT. One particular technique, *motivational interviewing*, is a style of questioning used to explore the person's ambivalence about change and to capitalize on their motivation to change. Motivational interviewing was originally developed to help with problematic alcohol use but has since been applied across a broad range of areas. It recognizes the importance of empathizing with the person's current situation while also eliciting their ambivalence about change. A basic tenet underlying CBT is that the individual probably wouldn't be where they are without good reason, so there will be pros and cons to any change. CBT therapists avoid getting drawn into telling the person what to do or arguing with them, instead they focus on their motivation for change, and enable them to develop their self-efficacy in making and sustaining behaviour change.

A related area is the use of CBT in treating addictive behaviour or substance misuse. The most obvious applications have been to the problematic use of alcohol and drugs, but similar techniques have been applied to non-substance-related behaviours such as gambling, excessive shopping, or even hoarding behaviours. At a basic level, CBT conceptualizes addictive behaviours as maladaptive attempts at coping with difficult feelings or circumstances. The general pattern of such behaviours is that they are rewarded in the short term by a high or some form of satisfaction, as well as by the avoidance of negative emotions or alleviation of uncomfortable physiological states. But in the longer term they create more problems than they solve, such as debt, relationship difficulties, cravings, and health problems. This is compounded by physiological dependence on a substance, where the person experiences withdrawal or other aversive states in the absence of the substance. This of course acts as a powerful reinforcer—the substance reduces the aversive withdrawal symptoms thereby rewarding the behaviour of using the substance.

As in all forms of CBT, CBT for addictive behaviours begins with an idiosyncratic formulation of the individual's difficulties that includes both the short- and longer term consequences of the behaviour. Then the therapist and patient will collaborate to identify and test out ways of breaking the cycles maintaining the unwanted behaviour. This may involve interventions such as skills training—for example, in assertive communication or problem solving. Or it may involve more standard CBT techniques such as challenging thoughts relating to the substance (e.g. 'I need it'; 'I will never enjoy anything again if I don't use'). Behavioural management techniques to deal with triggers can also be used. For instance exposure and response prevention whereby the patient is gradually exposed to a hierarchy of triggering situations, without responding by using the substance. Instead they may use relaxation techniques to reduce arousal or engage in behaviours that are incompatible with the addictive behaviour. Similar techniques are used in CBT for habit disorders. In trichotillomania (hair pulling) patients will experiment with behaviours that are incompatible with hair pulling such as keeping hair tied back, wearing a hat, or keeping their hands on their lap. This is especially useful for habits that are done with limited conscious awareness (e.g. nail biting). As in substance use, CBT for habit disorders seeks to formulate what function(s) the behaviour serves. Is it a form of self-soothing? If so what other, less harmful, methods could the patient use to self-soothe? Similarly, if the addictive behaviour serves to alleviate boredom or occurs in response to other negative emotional states, the patient can learn to use other methods for achieving those aims.

The maintenance of treatment gains is a particular challenge in working with addictions and habit disorders. Accordingly, CBT interventions prioritize maintenance strategies, and relapse prevention and management. This involves consideration of, and careful planning for, high risk situations. As in serious mental illness, it can be useful to identify the individual's typical pattern of relapse, their *relapse signature*, so that they can develop a plan for how to intervene to change course once they notice the early warning signs. For example, one patient with a history of chronically relapsing alcohol use identified the early warnings signs—of feeling increasingly stressed by work, withdrawing from their partner, and stopping engaging in self-care activities such as exercise—as changes that typically preceded a relapse. In response, they developed a plan to view these as warning signs and to take aversive action by: employing other skills to deal with the work stress; being open about the stress he was experiencing with both their employer and their partner; and, if necessary, taking time off from work and focusing on self-care. Equally important was learning to set appropriate boundaries and to ask for help so that they were at less risk of being overwhelmed at times of stress at work.

A further health-related area to which CBT has been successfully applied is in eating pathology. The three most common eating disorder diagnoses are *anorexia nervosa*, *bulimia nervosa*, and *binge eating disorder*, with less common issues being *pica* (eating non-food substances) and *avoidant/restrictive food intake disorder* (eating only a very restricted range of foods). Early CBT approaches to eating disorders concentrated on behavioural interventions focused on weight gain and normalizing eating patterns, sometimes using behavioural management strategies such as rewarding weight gain or removing privileges for a lack of weight gain in cases of anorexia. However, patients struggled to maintain the gains made in treatment outside of a controlled environment, possibly because underlying beliefs had not been addressed. More recently, CBT therapists such as psychiatrist Chris Fairburn and colleagues have developed versions of CBT that give more attention to the underlying cognitive elements, as well as eating-related behaviours. Anorexia, bulimia, and binge eating are seen as sharing important common maintaining mechanisms despite having distinctive features. For example, common to all three are disordered patterns of eating and placing excessive value on body shape and weight. Thus CBT for eating disorders focuses on breaking the common maintaining cycles such as overly restrictive eating patterns leading to rebound overeating and a perception of loss of control, as well as challenging beliefs overvaluing shape and weight (e.g. 'I can't be happy unless I achieve a certain weight'; 'nobody will respect me unless I am thin'). This approach has been successful across different types of eating disorders as well as with younger patients, and has been used with those who are significantly underweight. Results have been positive with treatment duration being forty sessions for those who begin treatment significantly underweight and twenty session for those who do not.

Serious mental illnesses

As well as being used to treat the more common mental health problems such as anxiety, depression, and addictions, CBT has been adapted for the treatment of serious mental illnesses. The term 'serious mental illness' refers to conditions characterized by a loss of contact with reality, such as *bipolar disorder* (previously called *manic depression*) or psychotic disorders such as *schizophrenia*. Hallmark symptoms of schizophrenia are the experience of *hallucinations* (false perceptions) and/or *delusions* (false beliefs) as well as a range of symptoms affecting mood and behaviour such as disorganized behaviour, lethargy, and the absence of emotion. While it is normal to experience a range of mood states from high to low, bipolar disorder is characterized by extreme swings of mood. The periods of high mood, called *manic episodes*, are when the person typically becomes overly optimistic, active, and driven, often in a way that leads to negative consequences such as excessive spending or inappropriate sexual activity. In a manic state the person is full of energy, often spilling over into irritability. They may be easily distracted and have little need for rest or sleep. This may lead to grandiose plans and thinking that becomes out of line with reality, as in delusions. For example, delusions of grandeur such as believing themself to be an especially important person or bestowed with special powers. Manic episodes are usually time limited, and in between manic episodes the person may have normal mood levels or, more typically, they may experience depressed mood, sometimes to a severe level.

Causes of serious mental illness are unclear, but they are likely to be multi-faceted and involve genetic vulnerabilities, changes in brain chemistry, as well as adverse life experiences including trauma. Historically the primary line of treatment has been anti-psychotic or mood stabilizing medication, both of which have been shown to have therapeutic effects but also significant adverse side effects. Because of the multi-faceted aetiology of serious mental illnesses, CBT approaches have generally not been used to aim to cure the disorder, but rather to help the patient to manage their illness as much as possible, to limit the impact of the symptoms, and to reduce the frequency and/or severity of episodes.

This has led to several different strands of intervention in CBT for serious mental illness. The first is the adaptation of standard CBT interventions for this population. For example, utilizing the mood management techniques typically used in CBT for depression or anxiety or trauma focused CBT. These interventions can be used effectively with patients experiencing serious mental illness but may require adaptations such as having shorter, more frequent sessions for those with concentration difficulties. Alternatively, CBT interventions in serious mental illness can focus on enhancing medication compliance. Barriers to complying with medication can be practical (e.g. the cognitively impaired patient who struggles to remember to take their tablets) or perceptual. Perceptual barriers include beliefs reflecting a lack of acceptance of the need for medication or benefits it brings (e.g. not taking anti-psychotic medication once they start feeling better). Recent research suggests that patients' compliance in taking medications can be improved by training their healthcare providers in cognitive behavioural change techniques.

A further application of CBT in serious mental illness has been to intervene directly on the symptoms that are specific to serious mental illness. For example, clinical psychologist Daniel Freeman has developed cognitive behaviour techniques for working with paranoia. Similarly, cognitive behavioural approaches to working with delusions and hallucinations, and the distress associated with them, have been proposed. Given CBT's inherent focus on the therapist questioning the patient's version of reality, when working with patients who have hallucinations or delusions it is even more important that any challenging of such beliefs is grounded in (i) a solid therapeutic relationship, and (ii) comprehensive shared formulation of the patient's difficulties. From this base the therapist can move on to introduce the idea that there may be more than one way of understanding their experience. For example, Theory A is that the voices are God speaking directly to the patient, whereas Theory B is that they are auditory hallucinations which are a product of the person's own mind, caused by their illness. The patient is then encouraged to compare the evidence for and against these two competing theories, and eventually to carry out behavioural experiments to generate evidence to discriminate between them. The idea being that if the voices are attributed to the illness rather than an omnipotent being they may be less distressing and may be responded to in more helpful ways—for example, by feeling less compelled to act on the voices and less fearful about not acting on them. Similar reattribution techniques have been used in working with paranoia and persecutory delusions with encouraging result in initial trials. Virtual reality has been useful in such interventions to enable patients to recreate imagined scenarios and practise newly developed skills in virtual environments.

In bipolar disorder, CBT interventions have had most impact by concentrating on relapse prevention in this typically episodic disorder. This is done by identifying an individual's *relapse signature*, that is their typical pattern of relapse into either mania or depression, and intervening to circumvent the deterioration or escalation of mood. Mood and activity monitoring are used to detect the early warning signs of a relapse and action is taken to reduce the pattern of mood escalation or deterioration. For example, increasing anti-depressant medication in response to lowered mood. Or recognizing early warning signs of a manic episode such as reduced need for sleep, and taking action to break the maintenance cycles such as reducing activity and resting more, limiting goal directed activity, or challenging grandiose thinking. CBT interventions in bipolar disorder have also targeted thinking or attribution styles that are believed to facilitate mood swings (e.g. black and white thinking, where things are seen as all good or all bad) and exaggerated interpretations of success or failure.

This chapter has covered a broad range of areas to which CBT has been applied, from anxiety disorders and trauma to addictions, eating disorders, and serious mental illness. Before concluding we will look at two further areas in which CBT has been used that are not considered 'disorders' or illnesses: anger and relationship difficulties.

Anger

Like fear or sadness, anger is not a disorder. Rather, it is an emotion which is more or less functional depending on the intensity, frequency, context, and way in which it is expressed. Anger that erupts too often or intensely, or that leads to behaviour that is unhelpful, damaging, or distressing (to the individual or others), can be a target for intervention. Cognitive behavioural conceptualizations of anger are based on the idea that anger is triggered when an individual perceives that their rules, for the way that the world should be, have been transgressed. For example, 'he didn't treat me with the respect I deserve' or 'life shouldn't be this difficult'. It is also recognized that anger can be a defensive reaction, in that it 'blocks' the experience of more distressing emotions such as sadness or fear—focusing on how you have been wronged may help to avoid having to confront your fears about why you weren't treated as well as you would have liked. Hence, CBT approaches to anger are multi-component. One of the first components is likely to be establishing motivation. Given the above ideas that anger is closely related to the individual's 'rules for living' or personal standards, and may serve to avoid the experience of more distressing emotions, it is likely that there may be ambivalence about change. Hence a useful starting point can be to look at the advantages or payoffs of anger, and the pros and cons of change. For example, in the case example on pp. 34–5, Neil noticed that his angry, aggressive outbursts had some benefits in the short term in that they brought an end to his wife's criticism of him, and allowed him to vent his frustration at the situation. However, they had more disadvantages than advantages, as they made him feel worse about himself and only exacerbated his wife's disapproval of him. Doing a thorough cost-benefit analysis can be particularly important where the individual has been referred for treatment (e.g. in court mandated referrals) because their anger is causing problems for others in, say, aggressive behaviour, as opposed to when someone has sought help for themselves because their anger is causing them suffering. Once motivation for change is established CBT interventions focus on anger control strategies such as stress inoculation training which was adapted by clinical psychologist Raymond W. Novaco for use with anger.

Stress inoculation training, applied to anger, involves three main stages. First is the preparation stage, which focuses on conceptual education. Here the patient learns to identify triggers and patterns of anger, including typical thoughts, feelings, behaviours, and physiological responses. They then go on to look at the advantages and disadvantages of anger (or of behavioural expressions of anger) and establish the motivation to change. The preparation stage concludes by devising a hierarchy of anger provoking situations, from the least to the most triggering. Following on from the preparation stage is skills acquisition and consolidation, which means learning skills to respond differently in anger provoking situations—learning to respond rather than react. This involves learning strategies and skills, such as taking time out, using relaxation to reduce arousal, or learning skills in assertive communication to express their views appropriately. Cognitive skills may also be learned in order to challenge anger triggering thoughts (e.g. unrealistic expectations of others / the world; blaming interpretations) and instead to identify alternative self-instructional statements that reduce rather than inflame anger (e.g. 'getting angry won't help—it hurts me more than anyone else'; 'I can't control others' behaviour, but I can control how I respond to it'). The final stage of stress inoculation training is to apply the skills across situations, so to practise their skills for reducing anger and arousal in a hierarchy of progressively more anger provoking situations. Often the skills are practised in roleplays with the therapist first, before moving on to working up a hierarchy of exposure in real life situations. It is important that the patient evaluates the outcome of responding differently in anger provoking situations and incorporates this reflection into future planning; and also that they identify high risk situations in advance and rehearse coping strategies. In some but not all cases, it may then be useful to look at working on residual or underlying beliefs (e.g. 'letting people get away with this means I'm weak'; 'if I don't kick off now and again people will take advantage'), and to identify any emotions that were avoided through being angry and consider whether they need to be a focus of intervention—for example, if they stop being angry at the world for the way it has treated them, they may need to process a lot of sadness or loss at those events that they had previously been angry about.

CBT approaches to anger have been applied across a range of patient groups including those in forensic services as well as those with intellectual disabilities. Outcomes have generally been positive, with reductions in self-reported experiences and expressions of anger. However, longer term outcomes are more variable and difficult to assess, and it is clear that anger remains a challenge in prisons.

Relationship difficulties

Like anger, relationship difficulties do not constitute a disorder. However, relationship problems do cause individuals significant distress, as well as having implications for families and children. Hence, relationship difficulties have become an area that psychological interventions have been applied to. People may seek help directly to focus on their relationship, or it may be that relationship work is identified as potentially useful when the formulation suggests that relationship issues may be contributing to an individual's difficulties.

CBT for relationship issues utilizes standard CBT techniques, but the focus is more on improving communication and aligning partners' expectations, as well as on developing problem solving skills. The types of beliefs identified as important targets for change in CBT for relationship problems are mismatched standards and expectations; unhelpful attributions of the other's behaviour; and poor communication skills. As with other versions of CBT, it is important to understand the developmental context of the relevant beliefs—that is, where they came from. For instance, childhood experiences from a person's family of origin are likely to influence their expectations in a relationship (e.g. believing that a good wife always puts her husband's needs first).

However, insight about the origins of a belief is unlikely to be sufficient to produce change. Instead, CBT focuses on improving communication, aligning expectations, and active problem solving. Partners may be operating with incompatible belief systems (e.g. 'in a happy relationship we should spend all out time together' vs 'to be a content adult, I need a degree of autonomy and time to myself'). The therapist may then explore whether the beliefs can be modified to something that both partners can live with. A further focus may be on modifying unhelpful attributions of blame (e.g. 'they don't pick up after themselves because they don't care about my needs') by challenging them. Instead couples are encouraged to share responsibility for the issues, and to specifically define the problem(s) and experiment with different solutions, without blame or recriminations.

As well as attempting to change beliefs, CBT for relationship difficulties utilizes skills training, such as effective communication, problem solving, and behavioural techniques (e.g. increasing the frequency of positive behaviours such as giving compliments or doing something positive for their partner). Sessions normally involve both partners but the assessment is likely to include at least some individual time. Furthermore, there may be circumstances in which individual therapy may be combined with or run concurrently with couples therapy. The individual therapy would focus on one partner's issues while the joint sessions would focus on the relationship. This is especially useful where issues may be related—for instance, a history of sexual trauma causing problems in the physical side of the current relationship; or anxiety and reassurance seeking impacting on the power balance in a relationship.

One criticism of CBT has been that it is only suitable for anxiety/depression with articulate adults who are psychologically minded and able to reflect on their problems. While CBT was originally developed for anxiety or depression, this chapter has aimed to show the broad range of problem areas or types for which CBT has been adapted and to which it has been applied. In addition to being adapted for different presenting problems, CBT approaches have been modified for working with different types of patients. Although initially developed for use with adults of normal intelligence, CBT has been adapted for use across a wide age and intellectual ability range. Adaptations have been made to the content and the process of CBT for specific populations—for example, having shorter sessions with more reliance on written materials for those with memory difficulties; or using drawings or audio/video recordings for those with lower levels of literacy. Much success has been had in simplifying CBT constructs for younger patients or those with intellectual disabilities. In addition, CBT approaches have also been successfully used in involving family members or carers across a range of patient groups (e.g. in helping parents to manage a child's challenging behaviour; or in engaging a partner to monitor relapse warning signs such as disrupted sleep patterns for a patient with bipolar disorder).

Chapter 7
Future directions and challenges

So far, we have focused on what might be called traditional, or Beckian, CBT—developed more or less directly from Beck's cognitive model of emotional disorder. As outlined in Chapter 1, early CBT focused on theories of learning—classical conditioning and operant learning. This is known as *first wave* CBT, with the *second wave* focusing more on thoughts and information processing elements. Both first and second wave versions of CBT are based on the premise that thoughts, feelings, physiological states, and behaviour are interlinked, so changing any one aspect will give rise to changes in the other aspects. Often the target for change is thoughts, as these have such a central role in the model, and are believed to be more directly amenable to change than, for example, physiology or emotion. However, a criticism of CBT is that we know very little about which of CBT's components is responsible for bringing about the change. Experimental studies have yielded mixed results, leading Longmore and Worrell to ask 'Do we need to challenge thoughts in cognitive behavior therapy?' *Dismantling trials* and *component analyses* have been used to investigate whether cognitive change (changing thoughts) is necessary for CBT to be effective in bringing about symptom relief. CBT interventions typically incorporate multiple components and dismantling trials or component analyses try to separate out and compare the effect of the different components. For example, a version of CBT for depression focusing solely on the behavioural components (*behavioural activation*) was found to be just as effective as the more complete version which included cognitive strategies to counter depressive thinking. Several subsequent studies have compared different components of CBT, or CBT with and without one specific component, with varying results. While Longmore and Worrell's early review concluded that 'component analyses have failed to show that cognitive interventions provide significant added value to the therapy', more recent reviews, by Cuijpers et al., have been more measured, noting how difficult it is to accurately evaluate the separate components of CBT, and concluding that 'currently available component studies do not have the statistical power nor the quality to draw any meaningful conclusion about key ingredients of psychotherapies for adult depression'. So the current evidence does not enable us to easily discern which are the most effective, or even necessary, components of CBT.

In recent years, several theoretical models suggest that more than changing the content of thoughts is required. It has long been been recognized that there can be a head vs heart discrepancy, whereby the patient knows intellectually that their fear is unrealistic but this is not enough to stop them from feeling afraid. As far back as 1995 an alternative was proposed to the idea that CBT was effective because it changed the content of cognitions. It was hypothesized that CBT may have its impact by helping the patient to be able to stand back, or decentre, from their thoughts—that is, by facilitating *metacognitive* awareness, which is the realization that thoughts are just thoughts, not necessarily valid reflections of reality. And in turn, metacognitive awareness may reduce the individual's reactivity to their thoughts.

It is against this background of questioning the relative contribution of changing thoughts that *third wave* CBT approaches have been proposed. Third wave CBT approaches aim to enhance the effectiveness of first and second wave CBT by emphasizing contextual and experiential change strategies. Third wave CBT encompasses a broad church of approaches, many of which have evolved independently of each other. What unites them is that they differ from traditional CBT in that, rather than encouraging patients to change the content of their thoughts in order to better manage feelings, physiological responses, and behaviour, they are encouraged to change their relationship with their thoughts. Thoughts are noticed and accepted as private mental events, especially the aversive or unwanted ones. This acceptance then reduces experiential avoidance. Early evaluations suggest several versions of third wave CBT approaches can be effective, despite the absence of the traditional focus on changing the content of cognitions.

Acceptance and commitment, and mindfulness based therapies

One of the earliest third wave approaches arose from the work of American psychologist Steven Hayes (1948–) who proposed *relational frame theory*, which is a behavioural analysis of language and cognition. This theory proposes that the foundation of human language, and therefore thought, is *relating*. That is, the ability to create links or associations between things. Previously classical conditioning (also called associative learning) had focused on the strength of associations between things, particularly stimuli and responses. In contrast, relational frame theory asserts that it is not just the strength of the association that is important, but the type of association (relation), as well as the dimensions along which the stimuli are related. Relational frame theory has formed the basis for the development of the third wave CBT approach known as *acceptance and commitment therapy* (ACT). ACT is based on the idea that psychological suffering is caused by:

- experiential avoidance—if we fear something, we avoid it, which prevents us from finding out if our fears are unfounded, and deprives us of opportunities for learning and skill development;

- cognitive entanglement—that we get tangled up in our own thoughts and ruminate rather than focusing on the broad range of information available through our senses; and
- a lack of psychological flexibility—which means that we fail to act in accordance with our core values.

ACT uses the acronym FEAR to explain psychological suffering, proposing that difficulties are caused by: *f*usion with your thoughts, *e*valuation of your experience; *a*voidance of your experience; and *r*eason giving for your behaviour. The healthy alternative to FEAR is ACT: *a*ccept your reactions and be present; *c*hoose and commit to a valued direction; and *t*ake action in the direction of your chosen values. ACT is based on behavioural psychology and utilizes interventions that manipulate reinforcers (rewards and punishments) to bring about changes in behaviour. In addition, it uses acceptance and mindfulness processes to promote psychological flexibility, and to develop commitment to valued goals and the behaviour change process. The six core principles shown in the box underlie the therapeutic techniques used in ACT.

Like many theories of information processing, ACT hypothesizes that there are two *modes of mind* or information processing systems. One mode is the discrepancy-based, problem solving system that facilitated our evolution into the dominant species. This system notes the discrepancy between our current state and our desired state and seeks to reduce that discrepancy. This works very well for states such as hunger, which can be directly reduced by the behaviour of eating. However, it works less well for aversive emotions—simply trying to be less fearful or sad may only strengthen the feeling, for example, by creating fear of fear, or hopelessness about depression. A good example is the paradoxical effect of thought suppression—if you close your eyes and try very hard not to think about a pink rabbit you are more likely to be distracted by rabbit-related thoughts than if you weren't actively trying not to think about rabbits. Counterintuitively, the more you try to reduce or escape from aversive emotions, the more they persist. And the effort of trying to escape from them, usually by avoidance, and the limitations that it brings with it, can be costly and disabling.

The other mode of mind is the experiential mode, which focuses on noticing, with curiosity, what is being experienced, both within and outside the body. ACT's intervention strategies seek to engage and strengthen the experiential mode through values-based practices, and acceptance and mindfulness strategies. ACT recognizes that the desire to avoid aversive emotional states is a natural one, shared across species, and is influenced by the sociocultural context. For example, Western cultures value states such as happiness, peace, and confidence. In contrast other sociocultural context are more accepting of negative emotional

Core principles of ACT

- Cognitive defusion: Learning methods to reduce the tendency to experience mental events (thoughts, images, emotions, memories) as absolute reflections of reality.

- Acceptance: Allowing thoughts to come and go without struggling to control them.

- Staying in the present moment: Awareness of the here and now, experienced with openness, interest, and receptiveness.

- Observation of the self: Experiencing a transcendental sense of self and a continuity of consciousness.

- Values: Identifying what values and goals are most important to one's true self.

- Committed action: Setting goals according to values and pursuing them responsibly.

29. Emotional avoidance detour.

states. For example, Buddhists view suffering as an integral and essential part of the human experience and do not seek to avoid it. Avoiding the experience of aversive emotional states may perpetuate suffering by preventing change and distracting you from progressing towards your value-based goals, as depicted in Figure 29. ACT sees values and pain as two sides of the same coin. You cannot have one without the other. Anything that is meaningful to you, whether it be your family, career success, or support for a football team, also has the potential to bring suffering and pain. In order to have the life that corresponds to what we value, we must be willing to experience the full range of emotions, including painful ones such as loss, fear, and sadness.

ACT aims to increase psychological flexibility and reduce emotional avoidance. One of the ways that it does this is by encouraging the patient to differentiate between what is and what is not, under their control. Real life problems, that occur outside the body, such as being hungry or cold, are often under our control, and with directed effort we can resolve them. However, aversive emotional states are often not amenable to our efforts to control them, and may even be exacerbated by attempts to control or avoid them. So ACT encourages the patient to recognize that they cannot control their inner emotional experience, but can approach it with curiosity and mindfulness, and accept and tolerate it. ACT uses analogies such as the passengers on the bus to demonstrate this, and help the patient to refocus on their goals and act accordingly, regardless of distracting mental events.

This principle of accepting emotional experience is shared by other *mindfulness-based approaches*. Jon Kabat-Zinn, while working at the University of Massachusetts Medical School, was one of the first to incorporate therapeutic meditation practices into a psychological intervention. In his 1990 book *Full Catastrophe Living: Using the Wisdom of Your Body and Mind to Face*

The passengers on the bus exercise

The passengers on the bus is an exercise used in ACT to help patients decentre and to promote psychological flexibility. The patient is asked to imagine that they are driving a bus. The bus is headed towards their valued life goals. En route, passengers join or leave the bus. Some passengers are neutral, others are positive and encouraging. But some are critical, negative, distracting, or disruptive. These passengers may try to convince the patient to slow down or divert the bus in a different direction, so as not to be heading towards their valued goals. The therapist may even roleplay one of these passengers and ask the patient to practise how they want to respond. Do they stop the bus? Divert it? Give up? Get distracted by an argument to justify their route? Or continue towards their destination? Likewise with thoughts passing through our minds, we have a choice over how much attention we give to the various 'passengers on the bus', and how much we let them upset or divert us.

Stress, Pain, and Illness he incorporates mindfulness meditation practices into a stress reduction programme to help people deal with chronic pain, stress, and anxiety. Mindfulness is the quality of being present and fully engaged with the present. That is, with whatever we are currently doing or experiencing—free from distraction or judgement, and aware of our thoughts and feelings without getting caught up in them. This moment-to-moment (mindful) awareness can be trained through a variety of meditation practices, which are then be applied to everyday situations. The focus is on living in the present with acceptance of our current experience, whatever that may be.

Combining mindfulness with more traditional cognitive therapy methods may seem counterintuitive—how can you challenge your thoughts in traditional (second wave) CBT while also mindfully accepting them? You may not be able to do both simultaneously, but mindfulness-based cognitive therapy (MBCT) proposes that it is helpful to have both of these tools in your armoury, and then choose which to employ depending on the situation.

Like most CBT theories, MBCT is based on an underlying theory or theoretical model—the *interacting cognitive subsystems* model of information processing, which sees the mind as a product of interacting components. Each of these components receives information from the senses as well as from other components of the mind creating an interacting network within which recurring patterns are triggered in response to stimuli. It is hypothesized that those who have experienced depressive cycles have 'smoothed the path' to the thinking and feeling depressive rumination mode more than those who have not experienced depression, thereby increasing the likelihood that they will experience further episodes of depression. The recurring patterns of interaction between mental components have been called *modes of mind* and compared to the gears of an engine, in that each gear has a function and changes between them can be triggered automatically or intentionally. The changing of gears, or modes of mind, is likened to the deploying of attention—that while there is an automatic mode of reacting to a given situation, it can be overridden by an intentional recalibration. And, as with a vehicle, the mind can only be in one gear at a time. MBCT aims to help the person recognize when a mental gear, or mode of mind, is unhelpful so that they can choose then to disengage from it and shift to a more adaptive or helpful mode. Mindfulness is seen as a mode that is incompatible with the ruminative mode typical of depression, and thus can be useful in helping a person to shift out of a depressive mode of thinking.

MBCT is usually offered as an eight-week programme in which participants are taught to observe their thoughts and feelings through the repeated practice of intentionally returning attention to an object or a physical aspect of themselves, such as their breath or body sensations. Participants are taught how to cultivate direct experiential awareness and non-judgemental acceptance of whatever arises in each moment, including negative mood states that trigger anxiety and negative thinking. The cultivation of awareness through mindfulness practice enables participants to recognize when negative and ruminative responses are being triggered, which in turn facilitates a decentring from these patterns of thought by seeing them as mental events rather than absolute reflections of reality. In contrast to standard CBT, where the focus has traditionally been on changing the content of thoughts, MBCT focuses on fostering metacognitive awareness of thoughts as well as other mental events, and on the modification of metacognitive processes that have been maintaining unhelpful reactive or ruminative mind states.

MBCT was originally developed in response to the highly prevalent and chronically relapsing nature of depression. It has long been known that even when depression has remitted, most people who have suffered one episode of depression will go on to experience another episode. And the more episodes that you have experienced, the more likely you are to experience further episodes, with some studies finding that 80 per cent of those who have experienced two episodes of depression will go on to have further episodes. The recurring nature of depression and its high prevalence present a huge challenge in terms of the scale of treatment needed. Thus, MBCT was developed as a cost-effective class-based intervention designed to target the cognitive processes (e.g. rumination and high cognitive reactivity) rendering depressed individuals vulnerable to repeated relapse and recurrence. MBCT has been shown to reverse processes hypothesized to underlie depressive psychopathology and to reduce the risk of relapse at least as much as if the patient were instead continuing to take antidepressant medication. Although originally designed for depressed patients in remission, initial studies suggest that MBCT may be helpful for a broad range of mental health problems including bipolar disorder, generalized anxiety disorder, panic disorder, chronic fatigue syndrome, and psychosis, as well as chronic, treatment-resistant, and suicidal forms of depression (see the Further reading section for reviews on the efficacy of MBCT interventions).

Because third wave therapies are a relatively recent development, the evidence base to support their efficacy is at a relatively early stage. However, one systematic review and meta-analysis of sixty randomized controlled trials of ACT, including a total of 4,234 participants, found that while the evidence base for ACT was not yet well-established for any disorder, it is probably efficacious for chronic pain and tinnitus, and possibly efficacious for depression, psychotic symptoms, obsessive compulsive disorder, mixed anxiety, substance misuse, and work-related stress. Similarly, a systematic review and meta-analysis of MBCT included six randomized controlled trials of nearly 600 patients and found that MBCT significantly reduced the risk of relapse into depression. While initial trials of both ACT and MBCT have shown promising results, further methodologically robust trials are needed before we can be confident that such third wave approaches have similar effectiveness to more traditional CBT. A further stage for emerging CBT interventions such as ACT and MBCT is their dissemination—crossing the gap between being developed, often in an academic setting, to being widely used in routine clinical practice.

Dissemination of CBT interventions

Crossing the gap from efficacy trials to routine practice, or implementation science, is a challenge common to many novel psychological interventions. In some ways CBT can be considered a victim of its own success—its demonstrated efficacy in treating common mental health problems, together with economic analyses outlining the considerable costs to the state of untreated mental illness, have led governmental and professional organizations to advocate the widespread provision of CBT to the general population, not only in the UK but also in the USA and elsewhere. However, with some studies suggesting that up to 20 per cent of the population suffers from anxiety or depression in any given year, one of the biggest challenges for CBT implementation is the scale of the problem(s) that it is attempting to address. This challenge of increasing the provision of CBT has led to further evolution and adaptation of CBT.

One of the first and foremost responses to the identified unmet need of untreated mental health difficulties has been an attempt to increase or 'scale up' provision of CBT to the general public. For example, in 2008 the UK government committed to a large-scale initiative for Improving Access to Psychological Therapies (IAPT) within the UK's National Health Service. The psychological therapies provided are those that have significant research showing that they are effective and as such are considered to be 'evidence based'. While CBT is often the dominant therapy model, IAPT services are expected to offer patients a choice of other evidence-based psychological interventions too such as counselling and interpersonal therapy. The IAPT programme has expanded year on year and currently provides help for over 900,000 people with common mental health problems per year.

The goal is for half of those treated to meet the criteria for *recovery*, in that they move from scoring above the threshold for *clinical caseness* to scoring below it, following treatment. In addition, employment status is considered an outcome criterion, and thus attention is paid to facilitating a return to employment. While provision of CBT interventions on such a large scale is not without its challenges, IAPT recovery targets have largely been met, and many of those whose outcome does not meet the criteria for recovery nevertheless experience significant improvement.

IAPT services utilize a *stepped* or *matched care* model. That is a system of delivering and monitoring treatments so that the most effective, yet least resource intensive, treatment is offered first; only 'stepping up' to more intensive or specialist services as clinically required. To simplify service provision in this model, CBT interventions have been split into 'high' and 'low' intensity interventions. *High intensity* interventions are the standard CBT interventions discussed throughout this book, which are usually twelve to twenty sessions of formulation driven CBT, delivered by a fully trained CBT therapist to an individual patient. This is, however, a comparatively resource intensive intervention so it has been questioned whether lower intensities of CBT intervention may also be effective, particularly for those with mild to moderate problems. To provide such interventions, the new role of a *low intensity* CBT practitioner was created—this is a therapist who is not fully trained to deliver high intensity CBT interventions but is specifically trained to deliver lower intensity interventions to higher volumes of patients. Such practitioners are often call 'psychological well-being practitioners' to reflect their role in dealing with the more common mild to moderate mental health problems.

Low intensity CBT interventions

The primary goal of low intensity CBT interventions is the same as high intensity CBT—to employ cognitive and behavioural therapies to alleviate the patient's symptoms of psychological distress. What differentiates the approaches is the intensity of the methods used with the idea that using lower intensity approaches will mean that the same therapeutic resource can be made available to more patients, thereby increasing the availability of CBT interventions to those that need them. Relatedly, low intensity CBT also aims to increase the accessibility of CBT by reducing or removing barriers to accessing interventions. For example, by not requiring patients to attend face-to-face sessions. Instead interventions might be provided over the phone or via a computer. There are many different versions of computerized CBT (cCBT) ranging from computer programs that train you to make more positive interpretations of ambiguous scenarios, thereby facilitating the development of more positive thinking biases, to self-help education-based programmes that demonstrate and attempt to teach basic CBT skills such as mood monitoring and thought challenging. Indeed, traditional individual CBT can also be delivered via a computer which is especially useful for patients who may have difficulty in attending face-to-face appointments (e.g. in geographically dispersed populations; or for disabled people) or in situations where face-to-face contact has to be limited (e.g. as was the case during the Covid-19 pandemic). A different modification which does not necessarily reduce therapist time but may increase accessibility is the provision of intensive CBT interventions. For example, CBT for phobias that is carried out over a single day has been shown to be equally effective to CBT therapy carried out over several shorter weekly sessions. Similarly, several studies have shown that twelve to twenty hours of CBT delivered in one week is no less effective than when the sessions are delivered at weekly intervals. Such changes to the standard delivery protocol are useful for patients who may not be able to attend twelve to twenty weekly sessions but could attend every day for one week (e.g. because employment or travel limitations make weekly sessions over a longer duration impractical).

A second way in which accessibility can be increased is by using a lower intensity of therapist resource, for a greater number of patients. This can be done by providing briefer interventions—either fewer or shorter sessions; or by increasing the ratio of patients to therapist—as in group therapy. Lower intensity interventions are often supported by a greater use of written materials and self-help methods such as self-monitoring and worksheets. Some interventions may also involve video presentations of specific issues or skills demonstrations. In the low intensity model, the therapist's role is often more akin to that of teacher or facilitator whose role is to guide the patient's self-help or skill development, with comparatively less emphasis on the therapeutic relationship.

Self-help is one of the lowest intensity CBT interventions. At its core is the aim that the patient will use self-help materials to teach themself CBT skills with little or no therapist input. *Pure self-help* is where there is no therapist input, whereas *assisted self-help* is where some level of therapist support is provided. For example, brief meetings or telephone calls to check understanding of reading materials and problem solve any difficulties in using the methods. To reduce barriers to accessing treatment, therapeutic reading materials, also known as *bibliotherapy*, can be prescribed by a health worker so that they are free at the point of contact to the patient. One of the biggest advantages to self-help approaches is their cost-effectiveness and accessibility—no need to attend appointments and can be done in the patient's own time, whenever it is convenient. They may also appeal to people who don't want the stigma of formally accessing mental health services; and have the benefit of being under the patient's control, and promoting autonomy and independence. The evidence for the value of self-help versions of CBT is mixed, with some studies suggesting that some therapist input may be necessary for self-help to be effective. And there are limitations—to use bibliotherapy the individual must be literate and self-motivated, making it unlikely to be sufficient to meet the needs of those with more chronic, severe, and complex difficulties. Computerized versions of self-help CBT have also been developed such as 'Fearfighter' for anxiety and 'Beating the Blues' for depression.

Again the evidence for their effectiveness is mixed but it has been sufficient good for them to be recommended by the National Institute of Clinical Excellence in the UK.

Group therapies can be anything from a single therapist delivering a stress management workshop to hundreds of people to smaller therapeutic groups focusing on specific problems such as childhood sexual abuse. The structured, educational style of CBT lends itself to group settings in its use of elements such as agenda setting, learning of skills (e.g. activity scheduling or thought challenging), and use of homework tasks and feedback. As well as the increased efficiency in use of therapist time, delivering CBT in a group setting has other advantages too. Group members are usually supportive of each other and the fact that the group consists of patients with similar problems is therapeutic in itself—it makes participants aware that they are not the only ones with this problem, thus normalizing it, and potentially reducing stigma and shame. The group members may also be helpful sources of information for each other, being able to share not only their experiences but also details of coping strategies and resources they have found useful. Fellow group members can also be useful aides when conducting behavioural experiments (e.g. carrying out a survey of people's attitudes) or other therapy tasks where an aide is required. The challenges of delivering CBT group therapy are similar to those in providing any therapeutic group intervention. There is less opportunity for tailoring the intervention to the individual's specific presentation and idiosyncratic beliefs or behaviours; one way of overcoming this is for group participants to have individual formulations. Furthermore, group dynamics must be managed, as there is the potential for group members to have unhelpful impacts on each other, such as when one member dominates or is critical of others, or when group members struggle to relate helpfully to each other. Some individuals, for example those with significant social anxiety, may find group settings particularly challenging, or they may find the group setting inhibiting when it comes to disclosing personal information. Often group interventions are provided by two therapists to meet the additional challenges of managing group dynamics and to tailor the intervention to individuals' needs, while delivering the planned content of the sessions.

In terms of outcomes, the evidence for group CBT intervention efficacy varies across different types of problem and patient. As to whether they are cost effective it must be remembered that group sessions tend to be longer than the standard one-hour session; they often have more than one therapist; and they may require more therapist preparation and review time. Also dropout rates can be significant. While positive therapeutic outcomes are reported, effect sizes can be smaller, and it has been questioned whether those with more complex or severe symptoms may be better suited to individual treatment.

Self-help and group interventions are an integral component of stepped care models whereby the patient is offered the lowest intensity intervention first, and only 'stepped up' to a higher intensity intervention if that is not sufficient to resolve their difficulties. While this has obvious resource benefits in being an efficient use of services, it does run the risk that before someone gets the most potent version of CBT they have to fail at several lower intensity versions, thereby running the risk that they may give up on the approach before they have had the best opportunity to benefit from it. Hence services have moved towards *matched care* models whereby the therapist making the initial assessment aims to determine what level of intervention is likely to be the best match for a particular patient. This means that, if needed, they will start the treatment process at a higher 'step' than they would have done with the previous system.

Concluding remarks

This book has sought to provide an overview of what CBT is, what it does, how, for whom, and in what contexts. One of the main points is that CBT is not a single-cookbook therapy but instead encompasses a broad range of cognitive and behavioural approaches that have continued to evolve. While the earliest interventions focused on modifying observable behaviour, CBT grew to place more emphasis on thoughts and other cognitive processes. Most recently the third wave approaches have moved the focus away from the content of thoughts to the individual's relationship with their thoughts, and the processes underlying thinking. One of the driving forces behind CBT's evolution and its success has been its close links with empirical research. CBT embraces scientific evaluation both within and outside of the session, with therapists assessing the impact of individual therapeutic manoeuvres as well as evaluating the overall impact of CBT interventions in comparison to other treatments.

While CBT has been the 'fashionable therapy pants' of recent years, it must continue to evolve to meet ongoing and new challenges. The scale of mental health problems and relative cost of traditional therapy are prompting developments into lower intensity approaches that may reach broader audiences. Similarly, the scale of training the workforce required to roll out interventions has presented a challenge, with the most effective and efficient ways of training therapists and monitoring their competence becoming another area for future development. Related to this is determining how individualized CBT interventions need to be, with the ideal being an intervention that tackles what is common across most patients with that disorder without neglecting what is specific to a particular individual. A further area of interest is investigating how CBT interacts with psychotropic medications. Questions remain about the most effective combination of CBT and medication for the treatment of anxiety and depression. In addition, recent research has indicated that there may be a role for pharmacologically augmented interventions—that is, combining medication (targeting certain neurochemical systems) with particular CBT interventions (e.g. exposure), to enhance its effects in reducing anxiety. The empirical nature of CBT lends itself to generating data about the usefulness of such approaches and, if relevant, incorporating them into future versions of CBT. It must also be remembered that CBT is not the only psychological treatment that is supported by research evidence and that we know very little about the effective components of any psychological intervention, or which interventions suit which types of people or problems best.

References

Chapter 1: The behavioural origins of CBT

Aristotle (2009). *The Nicomachean Ethics*, trans. W. D. Ross, ed. L. Brown. Oxford: Oxford University Press.

Goethe, J. (1989). *Wilhelm Meister's Apprenticeship*, trans. E. A. Blackall in cooperation with Victor Lange. New York: Suhrkamp Publishers.

National Institute for Clinical Excellence (NICE) n.d. Guidelines. https://www.nice.org.uk.

Storr, A. (2001). *Freud: A Very Short Introduction*. Oxford: Oxford University Press.

Watson, J. B., and Rayner, R. (1920). Conditioned emotional reactions. *Journal of Experimental Psychology*, *3*, 1–14.

Cover Jones, Mary (1924). A laboratory study of fear: The case of Peter. *Pedagogical Seminary*, *31*, 308–15.

Wolpe, J. (1990). *The Practice of Behavior Therapy*. London: Pergamon Press.

Tortella-Feliu, M., Bornas, X., and Llabrés, J. (2008). Computer-assisted exposure treatment for flight phobia. *International Journal of Behavioral Consultation and Therapy*, *4*, 158–71.

Öst, Lars-Göran (1989). One-session treatment for specific phobias. *Behaviour Research and Therapy*, *27*, 1–7.

Skinner, B. F. (1938) *The Behavior of Organisms: An Experimental Analysis*. New York: Appleton-Century.

Thorndike, E. L. (1927). The Law of Effect. *The American Journal of Psychology*, *39*, 212–22.

Deci, E. L., Koestner, R., and Ryan, R. M. (1999). A meta-analytic review of experiments examining the effects of extrinsic rewards on intrinsic motivation. *Psychological Bulletin*, *125*, 627–68; discussion 692–700.

Fryer, R. (2011). Financial incentives and student achievement: Evidence from randomized trials. *Quarterly Journal of Economics*, *126*, 1755–98.

Chapter 2: Putting the 'C' into CBT

Köhler, W., and Winter, E. (1976). *The Mentality of Apes*. London: Routledge/Liveright Publishing Corporation.

Tolman, E. C. (1948). Cognitive maps in rats and men. *Psychological Review*, *55*, 189.

Bandura, A. (1977). Self-efficacy: Toward a unifying theory of behavioral change. *Psychological Review*, *84*, 191–215.

Ellis, A. (1957). Rational psychotherapy and individual psychology. *Journal of Individual Psychology*, *13*, 38–44.

Ellis, A. (1976). The biological basis of human irrationality. *Journal of Individual Psychology*, *32*, 145–68.

Beck, A. T. (1964). Thinking and depression: II. Theory and therapy. *Archives of General Psychiatry*, *10*, 561–71.

Chapter 3: The theory behind CBT

Shakespeare, William (1564–1616 author) (1954). *The Tragedy of Hamlet, Prince of Denmark*. London: The Folio Society.

Beck, A. T., Rush, J., Shaw, B., and Emery, G. (1979). *Cognitive Therapy of Depression*. New York: Guilford.

Beck, A. T. (1976). *Cognitive Therapy and the Emotional Disorders*. New York: Meridian.

Schwartz, B. (1986). *Diets Don't Work*. London: Columbus Books.

Alden, L. E., and Wallace, T. (1995). Social phobia and social appraisal in successful and unsuccessful social interactions. *Behavior, Research and Therapy*, *33*, 497–505.

Chapter 4: The style and structure of CBT

Rogers, C. (1957). The necessary and sufficient conditions of therapeutic personality change. *Journal of Consulting Psychology*, *21(2)*, 95–103.

Burns, T., and Burns-Lundgren, E. (2015). *Psychotherapy: A Very Short Introduction*. Oxford: Oxford University Press.

Kazantzis, N., Deane, F. P., Ronan, K. R., and L'Abate, L (eds.) (2005). *Using Homework Assignments in Cognitive Behavior Therapy*. New York: Routledge.

Kennerley, H., Kirk, J., and Westbrook, D. (2016). *An Introduction to Cognitive Behaviour Therapy: Skills and Applications*. London: Sage.

Kroenke, K., Spitzer, R. L., and Williams, J. B. (2001). The PHQ-9: Validity of a brief depression severity measure. *Journal of General Internal Medicine, 16(9)*, 606–13. doi:10.1046/j.1525-1497.2001.016009606.x.

Chapter 5: CBT methods

Gilbert, E. (2006). *Eat, Pray Love*. London: Bloomsbury.

Moore, M. T., and Fresco, D. M. (2012). Depressive realism: A meta-analytic review. *Clinical Psychology Review, 32(6)*, 496–509.

Schlup, L., and Whisenhunt, D. (eds.) (2001). *It Seems to Me: Selected Letters of Eleanor Roosevelt*. Lexington, KY: University Press of Kentucky.

Padesky, C. A. (1993). Socratic questioning: Changing minds or guiding discovery? Keynote address to European Congress of Behavioral and Cognitive Therapies, London, 24 September.

Confucius. *The Analects of Confucius: A Philosophical Translation*. New York: Ballantine Books, 1999.

Chadwick, P., Birchwood, M., and Trower, P. (1996). *Cognitive Therapy for Delusions, Voices, and Paranoia*. Chichester: Wiley, p.37.

Kennerley, H., Kirk, J., and Westbrook, D. (2016). *An Introduction to Cognitive Behaviour Therapy: Skills and Applications*. London: Sage.

Twain, M. (1996). *Tom Sawyer Abroad*. New York: Oxford University Press.

Engelkamp, J. (1998). *Memory for Actions*. Hove: Psychology Press, p. 139.

Eysenck, H. (1993). Forty years on: The outcome problem in psychotherapy revisited, pp. 3–22. In Thomas R. Giles (ed.), *Handbook of Effective Psychotherapy*. New York: Springer US.

Clark, D. M. (1986) A cognitive approach to panic. *Behaviour Research and Therapy*, 24, 461–70.

Clark, D. M. (1993). Cognitive mediation of panic attacks induced by biological challenge tests. *Advances in Behaviour Research and Therapy*, 15, 75–84.

Clark, D. M. (2004). Developing new treatments: On the interplay between theories, experimental science and clinical innovation. *Behaviour Research and Therapy*, 42, 1089–104.

Clark, D. M., Salkovskis, P. M., Hackmann, A., Wells, A., Ludgate, J., and Gelder, M. (1999). Brief cognitive therapy for panic disorder: A randomized controlled trial. *Journal of Consulting and Clinical Psychology*, 67, 583–9.

Ehlers, A., and Clark, D. M. (2000). A cognitive model of posttraumatic stress disorder. *Behaviour Research and Therapy*, 38, 319–45.

American Psychiatric Association (APA) (2013). *Diagnostic and Statistical Manual of Mental Disorders* (5th ed.). Arlington, VA: APA.

Ehlers, A., and Breuer, P. (1992). Increased cardiac awareness in panic disorder. *Journal of Abnormal Psychology*, 101, 371–82.

Grey, N., Salkovskis, P., Quigley, A., Clark, D. M., and Ehlers, A. (2008). Dissemination of cognitive therapy for panic disorder in primary care. *Behavioral and Cognitive Psychotherapy*, 36, 509–20.

Salkovskis, P. M., Clark, D. M., and Gelder, M. G. (1996). Cognition-behaviour links in the persistence of panic. *Behaviour Research and Therapy*, 34, 453–8.

Salkovskis, P. M. (2002). Empirically grounded clinical interventions: Cognitive behaviour therapy progresses through a multi-dimensional approach to clinical science. *Behavioural and Cognitive Psychotherapy*, 30, 3–9.

Rothbaum, B. O., Foa, E. B., Riggs, D. S., et al. (1992). A prospective examination of post-traumatic stress disorder in rape victims. *Journal of Traumatic Stress*, 5, 455–75.

Moorey, S., and Greer, S. (2011). *Oxford Guide to CBT for People with Cancer* (2nd ed.). Oxford: OUP.

Miller, W. R., and Rollnick, S. (1991). *Motivational Interviewing: Preparing People to Change Addictive Behavior*. New York: Guilford Press.

Dalle Grave, R., Calugi, S., Sartirana, M., and Fairburn, C. G. (2015). Transdiagnostic cognitive behaviour therapy for adolescents with an eating disorder who are not underweight. *Behaviour Research and Therapy, 73*, 79–82.

Fairburn, C. G., Cooper, Z., Doll, H. A., O'Connor, M. E., Bohn, K., Hawker, D. M.,...Palmer, R. L. (2009). Transdiagnostic cognitive-behavioral therapy for patients with eating disorders: A two-site trial with 60-week follow-up. *American Journal of Psychiatry, 166*, 311–19.

Fairburn, C. G., Cooper, Z., Doll, H. A., O'Connor, M. E., Palmer, R. L., and Dalle Grave, R. (2013). Enhanced cognitive behaviour therapy for adults with anorexia nervosa: A UK-Italy study. *Behaviour Research and Therapy, 51*, R2–8.

Freeman, D., Bradley, J., Antley, A., et al. (2016). Virtual reality in the treatment of persecutory delusions: Randomised controlled experimental study testing how to reduce delusional conviction. *British Journal of Psychiatry, 211*, 5.

Beck, R., and Fernandez, E. (1998). Cognitive-behavioral therapy in the treatment of anger: A meta-analysis. *Cognitive Therapy and Research, 22*, 63–74.

Novaco, R. (1975). *Anger Control: The Development and Evaluation of an Experimental Treatment.* Lexington, MA: D.C. Heath.

Chapter 7: Future directions and challenges

Longmore, R. J., and Worrell, M. (2007). Do we need to challenge thoughts in cognitive behavior therapy? *Clinical Psychology Review, 27*, 173–87, at 173.

Cuijpers, P., Cristea, I. A., Karyotaki, E., Reijnders, M., and Hollon, S. D. (2019). Component studies of psychological treatments of adult depression: A systematic review and meta-analysis. *Psychotherapy Research, 29*, 15–29, at 15.

Hayes, S., and Smith, S. (2005). *Get out of your mind and into your life: The new acceptance and commitment therapy.* Oakland, CA: New Harbinger publications.

Ost, L. G. (2014). The efficacy of Acceptance and Commitment Therapy: An updated systematic review and meta-analysis. *Behaviour Research and Therapy, 61*, 105–21.

Hargus, E., Crane, C., Barnhofer, T., and Williams, J. M. G. (2010). Effects of mindfulness on meta-awareness and specificity of describing prodromal symptoms in suicidal depression. *Emotion*, *10*, 34–42.

Kuyken, W., Byford, S., Taylor, R.S., et al. (2008). Mindfulness-based cognitive therapy to prevent relapse in recurrent depression. *Journal of Consulting and Clinical Psychology*, *76*, 966–78.

Kuyken, W., Hayes, R., Barrett, B., et al. (2015). The effectiveness and cost-effectiveness of mindfulness-based cognitive therapy compared with maintenance antidepressant treatment in the prevention of depressive relapse/recurrence: Results of a randomised controlled trial (the PREVENT study). *Health Technology Assessment*, *19*, 1–124.

Piet, J., and Hougaard, E. (2011). The effect of mindfulness-based cognitive therapy for prevention of relapse in recurrent major depressive disorder: A systematic review and meta-analysis. *Clinical Psychology Review*, *31*, 1032–40.

Raes F., Dewulf, D., Van Heeringen, C., and Williams, J. M. (2009). Mindfulness and reduced cognitive reactivity to sad mood: Evidence from a correlational study and a non-randomized waiting listcontrolled study. *Behaviour Research and Therapy*, *47*, 623–7.

Segal, Z. V., Bieling, P., Young, T., et al. (2010) Antidepressant monotherapy vs sequential pharmacotherapy and mindfulness-based cognitive therapy, or placebo, for relapse prophylaxis in recurrent depression. *Archives of General Psychiatry*, *67*, 1256–64.

Teasdale J. D., Segal Z., and Williams J. M. G. (1995). How does cognitive therapy prevent depressive relapse and why should attentional control (mindfulness) training help. *Behaviour Research and Therapy*, *33*, 25–39.

Teasdale, J. D., Segal, Z. V., Williams, J. M. G., Ridgeway, V. A., Soulsby, J. M., and Lau, M. A. (2000). Prevention of relapse/recurrence in major depression by mindfulness-based cognitive therapy. *Journal of Consulting and Clinical Psychology*, *68*, 615–23.

American Psychiatric Association (APA) (2013). *Diagnostic and Statistical Manual of Mental Disorders* (5th ed.). Arlington, VA: APA.

Davis, I., Thompson, E., Ollendick, T., and Öst, L. G. (2012). *Intensive One-Session Treatment of Specific Phobias*. New York: Springer-Verlag.

Ehlers, A., Hackmann, A., Grey, N., et al. (2014). A randomized controlled trial of 7-day intensive and standard weekly cognitive therapy for PTSD and emotion-focused supportive therapy. *American Journal of Psychiatry, 171,* 294–304.

Jacobson, N. S., Dobson, K. S., Truax, P. A., Addis, M. E., Koerner, K., Gollan, J. K., et al. (1996). A component analysis of cognitive-behavioral treatment for depression. *Journal of Consulting and Clinical Psychology, 64,* 295–304.

National Institute for Health and Care Excellence. Computerised cognitive behaviour therapy for depression and anxiety. 2006. https://www.nice.org.uk/guidance/TA97 (accessed 12 October 2016).

Further reading

Chapter 1: The behavioural origins of CBT

Burns, T., and Burns-Lundgren, E. (2015). *Psychotherapy: A Very Short Introduction*. Oxford: Oxford University Press.

Fryer R. (2011). Financial incentives and student achievement: Evidence from randomized trials. *Quarterly Journal of Economics*, *126*, 1755–98.

Giles, T. R. (ed.). (1993). Plenum behavior therapy series. *Handbook of Effective Psychotherapy*. London: Plenum Press.

Price, M., Anderson, P., and Rothbaum, B. O. (2008). Virtual reality as treatment for fear of flying: A review of recent research. *International Journal of Behavioral Consultation and Therapy*, *4*, 309–15.

Thorndike, E. (2017). *Animal Intelligence: Experimental Studies*. London: Taylor & Frances.

Chapter 2: Putting the 'C' into CBT

Beck, A. T. (1976). *Cognitive Therapy and the Emotional Disorders*. New York: Meridian.

Beck, A., Rush, J., Shaw, B., and Emery, G. (1979). *Cognitive Therapy of Depression*. New York: Guilford Press.

Ellis, A. (2004). *Rational Emotive Behavior Therapy: It Works for Me—It Can Work for You*. Amherst, NY: Prometheus Books.

Chapter 3: The theory behind CBT

Kennerley, Kirk J., and Westbrook, D. (2016). *An Introduction to Cognitive Behaviour Therapy: Skills and Applications.* London: Sage.

Myles, P., and Shafran, R. (2015). *The CBT Handbook: A Comprehensive Guide to Using Cognitive Behavioural Therapy to Overcome Depression, Anxiety and Anger.* London: Robinson.

Tarrier, N., and Johnson, J. (2016). *Case Formulation in Cognitive Behaviour Therapy: The Treatment of Challenging and Complex Cases.* London: Routledge.

Chapter 4: The style and structure of CBT

Beck, J. S., and Beck, A. T. (2021). *Cognitive Behavior Therapy: Basics and Beyond.* New York: Guilford Press.

https://www.padesky.com/clinical-corner/publications/

https://uk.cochrane.org/about-us

https://www.nice.org.uk/guidance

Chapter 5: CBT methods

Bennett-Levy, J., et al. (2010). *Oxford Guide to Behavioural Experiments in Cognitive Therapy.* Oxford: Oxford University Press.

Greenberger, D., and Padesky, C. A. (2016). *Mind over Mood: Change How You Feel by Changing the Way You Think* (2nd ed.). New York: Guilford Press.

Kennerly, H. (2020). *The ABC of CBT.* London: Sage.

McMillan, D., and Lee, R. (2010). A systematic review of behavioral experiments vs. exposure alone in the treatment of anxiety disorders: A case of exposure while wearing the emperor's new clothes? *Clinical Psychology Review, 30(5),* 467–78.

Padesky, C. A., and Greenberger, D. (1995). *Clinicians Guide to Mind over Mood.* New York: Guilford Press.

https://www.padesky.com/clinical-corner/

Chapter 6: Applications of CBT

Freeman, J., and Freeman, D. (2012). *Anxiety: A Very Short Introduction.* Oxford: Oxford University Press.

Freeman, D., and Freeman, J. (2020). *Paranoia: The Twenty-first Century Fear*. Oxford: Oxford University Press.

Freeman, D., Freeman, J., and Garety, P. A. (2016). *Overcoming Paranoid and Suspicious Thoughts: A Self-help Guide Using Cognitive Behavioral Techniques*. London: Robinson.

Jahoda, A., Kroese, B. S., and Pert, C. (2017). *Cognitive Behaviour Therapy for People with Intellectual Disabilities: Thinking Creatively*. London: Palgrave Macmillan.

Rollnick, S., and Miller, W. R. (2008). *Motivational Interviewing in Health Care: Helping Patients Change Behavior*. New York: Guilford Press.

Simos, G., and Hofmann, S. G. (2013). *CBT for Anxiety Disorders: A Practitioner Book*. Chichester: Wiley-Blackwell.

Steel, C. (2013). *CBT for Schizophrenia*. New York: John Wiley & Sons.

Steketee, G., and Frost, R. O. (2007). *Compulsive Hoarding and Acquiring: Therapist Guide*. Oxford: Oxford University Press.

White, D., Wright, M., Baber, B., and Barrera, A. (2018). A pilot study evaluating the effectiveness of a medicines education group in a mental health inpatient setting: A UK perspective. *Mental Health Clinic*, 7, 116–23.

Worrell, M. (2015). *Cognitive Behavioural Couple Therapy: Distinctive Features*. London: Routledge.

Chapter 7: Future directions and challenges

Bennett-Levy, J., Richards, D., Farrand, P., Griffiths, D. K., Klein, B., Proudfoot, J., and Ritterband, L. (2014). *Oxford Guide to Low Intensity CBT Interventions*. Oxford: Oxford University Press.

Gaudiano, B. A. (2008). Cognitive-behavioural therapies: Achievements and challenges. *Evidence Based Mental Health*, 11, 5–7.

Hayes, S. C. (2020). *A Liberated Mind: How to Pivot toward What Matters*. xy2: Avery (imprint of Penguin Random House LLC).

Hofmann, S. G., Sawyer, A. T., Witt, A. A., and Oh, D. (2010). The effect of mindfulness-based therapy on anxiety and depression: A meta-analytic review. *Journal of Consulting and Clinical Psychology*, 78, 169–83.

Kabat-Zinn, Jon. (2013). *Full Catastrophe Living: Using the Wisdom of Your Body and Mind to Face Stress, Pain, and Illness*. New York: Bantam Books.

Layard, R., and CEP Mental Health Policy Group. (2006). The Depression Report: A New Deal for Depression and Anxiety Disorders. CEP Special Papers 15, Centre for Economic Performance, LSE.

Mueller, M., Kennerley, H., McManus, F., and Westbrook, D. (2010). *Oxford Guide to Surviving as a CBT Therapist*. Oxford: Oxford University Press.

Rumi (2004). *Selected Poems*, trans. Coleman Barks with John Moynce, A. J. Arberry, and Reynold Nicholson. London: Penguin Books.

Segal, Z. V., Teasdale, J. D., and Williams, J. M. G. (2004). Mindfulness-based cognitive therapy: Theoretical rationale and empirical status, pp. 45–65. In S. C. Hayes, V. M. Follette, and M. M. Linehan (eds.), *Mindfulness and Acceptance: Expanding the Cognitive-Behavioral Tradition*. New York: Guilford Press.

Teasdale, J. D., and Barnard, P. J. (1993). *Essays in Cognitive Psychology. Affect, Cognition, and Change: Re-modelling Depressive Thought*. London: Lawrence Erlbaum Associates, Inc.

Warnock-Parkes, E., Wild, J., Thew, G., et al. (2020). Treating social anxiety disorder remotely with cognitive therapy. *The Cognitive Behaviour Therapist*, 13, E30.

Wild, J., Warnock-Parkes, E., Murray, H., Kerr, A., Thew, G., Grey, N., Clark, D. M., and Ehlers, A. (2020). Treating posttraumatic stress disorder remotely with cognitive therapy for PTSD. *European Journal of Psychotraumatology*, 11, 1–15.

Williams, M, and Penman, D. (2011). *Mindfulness. A Practical Guide to Finding Peace in a Frantic World*. Emmaus, PA: Rodale Books.

Index

THE HISTORY OF MEDICINE
A Very Short Introduction
William Bynum

Against the backdrop of unprecedented concern for the future of health care, this Very Short Introduction surveys the history of medicine from classical times to the present. Focussing on the key turning points in the history of Western medicine, such as the advent of hospitals and the rise of experimental medicine, Bill Bynum offers insights into medicine's past, while at the same time engaging with contemporary issues, discoveries, and controversies.

SLEEP
A Very Short Introduction
Russell G. Foster & Steven W. Lockley

Why do we need sleep? What happens when we don't get enough? From the biology and psychology of sleep and the history of sleep in science, art, and literature; to the impact of a 24/7 society and the role of society in causing sleep disruption, this *Very Short Introduction* addresses the biological and psychological aspects of sleep, providing a basic understanding of what sleep is and how it is measured, looking at sleep through the human lifespan and the causes and consequences of major sleep disorders. Russell G. Foster and Steven W. Lockley go on to consider the impact of modern society, examining the relationship between sleep and work hours, and the impact of our modern lifestyle.

www.oup.com/vsi

FORENSIC PSYCHOLOGY
A Very Short Introduction
David Canter

Lie detection, offender profiling, jury selection, insanity in the law, predicting the risk of re-offending, the minds of serial killers and many other topics that fill news and fiction are all aspects of the rapidly developing area of scientific psychology broadly known as Forensic Psychology. *Forensic Psychology: A Very Short Introduction* discusses all the aspects of psychology that are relevant to the legal and criminal process as a whole. It includes explanations of criminal behaviour and criminality, including the role of mental disorder in crime, and discusses how forensic psychology contributes to helping investigate the crime and catching the perpetrators.

www.oup.com/vsi

MEMORY
A Very Short Introduction
Michael J. Benton

Why do we remember events from our childhood as if they happened yesterday, but not what we did last week? Why does our memory seem to work well sometimes and not others? What happens when it goes wrong? Can memory be improved or manipulated, by psychological techniques or even 'brain implants'? How does memory grow and change as we age? And what of so-called 'recovered' memories? This book brings together the latest research in neuroscience and psychology, and weaves in case-studies, anecdotes, and even literature and philosophy, to address these and many other important questions about the science of memory - how it works, and why we can't live without it.

www.oup.com/vsi

GENIUS
A Very Short Introduction
Andrew Robinson

Genius is highly individual and unique, of course, yet it shares a compelling, inevitable quality for professionals and the general public alike. Darwin's ideas are still required reading for every working biologist; they continue to generate fresh thinking and experiments around the world. So do Einstein's theories among physicists. Shakespeare's plays and Mozart's melodies and harmonies continue to move people in languages and cultures far removed from their native England and Austria. Contemporary 'geniuses' may come and go, but the idea of genius will not let go of us. Genius is the name we give to a quality of work that transcends fashion, celebrity, fame, and reputation: the opposite of a period piece. Somehow, genius abolishes both the time and the place of its origin.

www.oup.com/vsi

STATISTICS
A Very Short Introduction
David J. Hand

Modern statistics is very different from the dry and dusty discipline of the popular imagination. In its place is an exciting subject which uses deep theory and powerful software tools to shed light and enable understanding. And it sheds this light on all aspects of our lives, enabling astronomers to explore the origins of the universe, archaeologists to investigate ancient civilisations, governments to understand how to benefit and improve society, and businesses to learn how best to provide goods and services. Aimed at readers with no prior mathematical knowledge, this *Very Short Introduction* explores and explains how statistics work, and how we can decipher them.

www.oup.com/vsi

NOTHING
A Very Short Introduction
Frank Close

What is 'nothing'? What remains when you take all the matter away? Can empty space - a void - exist? This *Very Short Introduction* explores the science and history of the elusive void: from Aristotle's theories to black holes and quantum particles, and why the latest discoveries about the vacuum tell us extraordinary things about the cosmos. Frank Close tells the story of how scientists have explored the elusive void, and the rich discoveries that they have made there. He takes the reader on a lively and accessible history through ancient ideas and cultural superstitions to the frontiers of current research.

'An accessible and entertaining read for layperson and scientist alike.'

Physics World

www.oup.com/vsi